D1545698

The Adult Orphan Club

First edition June 2020

Cover design by Vanessa Lovegrove
www.vanessalovegrove.co.uk

ISBN 978-1-8380635-1-1

For more information, visit www.florabaker.com

For Mum and Dad

"All the way round and back again"

Contents

For You

I'm so sorry that you're reading this. I know you're feeling scared, vulnerable and alone. Maybe you need to find a quiet place to breathe slowly. Maybe you're confused by how angry you are.

I know it hurts like hell, but I'm keenly aware that I don't know you. I don't know your unique story or your unique pain. Nobody truly can.

Words alone are not enough to help you get through this either – but you can still take comfort from the little things. That's still possible. So I'd like to try.

If you're feeling overwhelmed, try to remember that things will calm down eventually.

If you're sobbing so much that it feels like you might never stop, think of it like the tide. It comes right up to the edge, but it always falls back down again.

If you're feeling furious, ride that emotion like the biggest wave you've ever seen. Use the power of this thing you don't understand to pull yourself further forward.

I wish you didn't have to read these pages. But I'm so proud of you for deciding to seek out someone else's experience of grief. And I hope it helps you feel less alone in all this.

Because although it may feel like it, I promise that you are absolutely not alone.

You're not defeated.

You have love around you.

And you will get through this.

Introduction

At the age of thirty, I had no parents. I was orphaned and on my own. My mum died suddenly when I was twenty. My dad died slowly when I was twenty-nine. I have no siblings and no close family, so their deaths left me both bereaved and bereft. The realisation that I no longer had any 'real' family left was like a thunderbolt.

I've spent most of the last decade grieving, learning how to navigate this strange, life-altering loss, and working out how to enjoy my life.

It's not an easy thing to do.

Grief is active. Grief is lonely. Grief goddamn hurts. It's a physical, mental and emotional pain, the like of which is incomparable with anything else I've experienced. I've been totally consumed by grief, unable to leave my house for fear of being overwhelmed by unexpected emotion. And I've felt so lonely because of it.

One of the hardest things about grief is that there's

no rule book. It's completely up to you – your body, your mind, your emotions, and your intuition – to parse how to act, think, and feel your way through the grief-cloud. Your friends are supremely cautious about giving the wrong advice or adding any further stress, so they're gentle with everything they say to you. Much of the time I'd hear, "We can do whatever [it is] you want." But that's the problem. I had no bloody clue what I wanted. And what may feel like appropriate behaviour (i.e. spending your days sobbing on the carpet) is fundamentally flawed, because you've been through such huge trauma that your instincts are all over the place.

I've felt such internal pressure to "get better" – that it was expected of me – and yet I've never been closer to suicide either. Not because I wanted to die, but because I couldn't bear feeling this sad anymore. I didn't feel as if there could be any escape from it.

My world changed utterly when my parents died. Yet because grief is still such a taboo subject for most of us, there was an unspoken, unseen, yet monumental pressure to hide how I felt. You've either lost someone and felt this kind of grief or you haven't – and it can be really tricky to know how to behave.

But the truth is that the vast majority of us will have to face the death of our parents. I've just been confronted with the situation earlier in life than most.

Here's what I've learned about grief. First of all, there's no right or wrong way to grieve. Every person approaches this process differently – some seem to welcome it, others are dragged kicking and screaming by the volatility of their own emotions – but all of us will grieve eventually.

Grief cannot be cured.

Grief is not something you get over.

Grief doesn't just disappear.

There's no such thing as grieving too much, grieving for too long, or not grieving enough. But grief has some unexpected qualities too. It's at once a uniquely personal and unavoidably shared experience. Because however isolated and alone I've felt with this maelstrom of grief-emotions, I've still been able to find comfort in knowing that thousands – millions – of people have felt the same as me. And I've also learned that we simply *have* to experience grief ourselves to understand how best to move through it. It's the necessary recovery process of how we mentally and physically deal with the loss of a loved one. And how we figure out how to continue living without them.

Why I've written this book

There's a lot of practical advice out there from psychologists, therapists, grief experts, and bereavement professionals. I'm not one of them; I have no professional advice-giving qualifications. But I have lived through grief. I know it intimately. And I do feel able to share my story and what I've learned about grieving.

I've also spent unknown hours Googling every possible grief and death-related phrase, in the hope that I'd find something more personal and unique than generic lists of coping mechanisms and academic language. What I really wanted to find and read was personal experience. I wanted companionship on this journey through grief. I wanted to know that real people had been through what I'd been through, that they'd felt the way I felt, that they'd had the same sensation of their world being completely and utterly ripped apart. And honestly? I think I wanted to see other people's pain. Their fear and sadness. Their loneliness. I wanted to know that others had been in the same total darkness as me, but also that they'd faced that terrifying internal despair and still managed to make it through to the other side.

This book is intended for anyone who's grieving, but most of all it's for those of you who are coping with the loss of one parent or both. That's the situation I'm describing throughout these pages: this strange experience of your world's foundation being pulled from underneath you, and learning how to manage afterwards.

I've divided the book into four parts, each covering an aspect of the grief journey. *Part One: Grief Work* takes you through the initial shock of learning that someone is dying and what to do in the first weeks after they've died. I talk about the emotional responses likely to arise, the logistical decisions which need to be made, the questions to ask, and suggestions to make this difficult time somewhat easier. In *Part Two: Responses to Grief*, I explore all the emotional and physical ways that grief affects you. Learning to recognise situations which might trigger you and developing techniques to minimise their impact is a valuable skill – as is understanding that all your responses are valid, however confusing they might feel. *Part Three: Complicated Grief* talks about how to navigate the overwhelming aspects of grief. Whether you decide to reach out for professional help, rely on support from family and friends, or come up with sufficient self-care strategies to handle it yourself, these chapters will help you understand how to live alongside your grief. *Part Four: The Language of Grief* delves into how we talk about grief and death, why our choice of language is important, and what to say when helping someone through grief.

At the time of writing I'm thirty-two years old, and not

married nor in a long-term relationship. I have no children. I have no pets. It's been over ten years since my mum died, two years since my dad's death, and I live alone in the family house I grew up in, surrounded by my parents' possessions mixed in amongst my own.

I mention this so you understand that I know what it is to be alone as an adult orphan. And yet it's vital that you also understand that I'm happy again. It's a bittersweet kind of happiness, and I'll never be the person I was before my parents died, but that's OK. I honestly never thought I'd feel any different from the grief state I once lived in, but it really is possible.

This book is both a memoir and a guide to grieving. It's what happened to me when my parents died: an honest retelling of everything I faced and how I got from one day to the next.

This is the story of how I found my way through grief. I hope that reading it will help you handle your grief too.

PART ONE

–

GRIEF WORK

1

My Story

What do you do when your life falls apart? When it happened to me, I ran away.

I was twenty years old and midway through my second year of university when my mum called me to say her cancer was back. Despite a successful mastectomy and chemotherapy treatment ten years earlier in 1999, a few hidden cells lying dormant in her breast tissue had suddenly woken up. But the doctors had caught it quickly, she said, and they were already deciding on the best course of action. She was going to be fine.

And yet, on the night I came home for Christmas, my dad and I had to call an ambulance to take Mum to hospital. The doctors diagnosed the stroke which took away her speech, her emotions, and her mum-like

normality on December 18th; told us she was terminal on Christmas Eve and moved her to a hospice just before the new year began.

Mum died at 3 a.m. in a quiet room amidst the soft snow of early January 2008. We'd had just two weeks between learning she would die and watching as she took her last breaths. As Dad and I left the hospice that night, I knew my life would never be the same again – but I felt strangely distanced from the entire situation, as if it was happening to someone else. I know now that I must have been in shock. Two weeks is not enough time to comprehend such a monumental shift.

What I hadn't realised until she vanished from my life was my mum's irrefutable presence. A theatre actress by profession and a dramatic woman by nature, she was a constant whirlwind of energy, emotion, and positive attitude: a woman who befriended people in the queue at the post office, waved at every child she saw, and always had friends drinking cups of tea in the kitchen when I came home from school. She was fundamentally always there, in every sense of the word. Until she wasn't.

Mum had always been desperate to be involved in every aspect of my life – and although I relished it as a somewhat precocious child, when I became a teenager I'd found it stifling. Yet her death felt like a tap had been suddenly shut off. That gushing, never-ending flow of love, adoration, pride, and confidence in everything I ever did had disappeared. The impact was devastating in a way I never could have imagined. I physically felt the lack of her. My body ached for her. I was desperate to feel her hug me again. I dreamed about the sensation of touching her skin.

I'd never been particularly close to my dad. My parents didn't have much money when I was growing up, and Dad's job as a theatre director meant late nights spent at rehearsal studios or watching performances. When I was a child he'd get home when I was already tucked up in bed, and as I got older our personalities clashed. Dad was often quick to anger so I tended to keep my distance, maintaining a jokey, surface-level relationship with him. And besides, Mum was always the conduit between us. Thanks to her chatty nature, Dad and I never really engaged in long conversations together; he learned everything he needed to know about my life second-hand, from her.

Mum's death made it clear that we didn't know how to be a family without her. Dad and I stumbled through the days without really discussing what had happened. Our actions were considerate, though: cups of tea made for each other at odd hours, strange meals from the freezer when neither of us had much appetite, glasses of wine poured each evening without asking. A lot of sleeping, probably. In all honesty, I don't remember much, except how silent and empty the house felt. Yet somehow we managed to organise a funeral in the freezing January weather, filling a church with mourners still stunned with shock. I stood at the lectern and felt a strange pride in managing to deliver a eulogy for my beautiful, wonderful mum. We held the wake at a pub near our house, and despite a merrily-burning fire and plenty of people wanting to hug me, I quickly felt suffocated by it all and half-ran through the streets towards the safety of home.

I went back to university a few days after the funeral, and the blurred months moved past: lectures which I couldn't focus on, a student union job I had to quit, and nights spent smoking weed with my boyfriend while we played Lego Indiana Jones on his Playstation. When I drank, I drank a lot. Nights out vanished from my mind; I would drink and be happy until a certain point, then I would crumble. My friendship circles tightened, closing ranks to keep me safe. Dad and I began speaking often on the phone, and I took the train back to London most weekends. He cooked us the meals Mum had loved: beef bourguignon, chilli con carne, prawn and coconut curry with homemade cucumber raita. Before I left the house he'd press Tupperware boxes of leftovers into my hands.

When I was alone in my university bedroom, I sat

up at night sobbing into the wallpaper. I screamed at a stranger in the student union when she spilt her drink on my shoes, and in the middle of a lecture about American poetry, I broke down and ran out to cry in a toilet stall. It felt like my mind was no longer my own.

Eight months after Mum's death I flew to the USA to study in San Francisco for the year abroad portion of my degree. I'd been accepted into San Francisco State University just before she died, and we'd discussed this around Mum's hospital bed while she had an unexpected moment of lucidity: "You can't let this stop you going to America, Flor!" she said. It was enough to bolster my decision to leave Dad behind and head somewhere completely different. I'd always loved travelling – my parents had both spent their lives working in theatre productions all over the world, so it was in my blood – but I wasn't expecting the sense of relief I felt at being in a country which didn't remind me of Mum. In London, I would see her hair in a crowd of people, hear her voice in a supermarket, or be struck dumb by her hand clutching the yellow railing of a tube train. In San Francisco, I didn't see the ghost of her anywhere. It was the closest thing to a holiday from the constant presence of grief.

The downside was not being near anyone who knew me from "before". An eight-hour time difference and thousands of miles separated me from my dad, my close friends and my boyfriend – a relationship which was quickly destroyed by being long-distance and which, at the time, felt akin to losing my mum all over again.

I was furious a lot of the time in San Francisco. The tiniest things triggered me, but I was numb too. A sense of watching my life happen to someone else still dogged me. I found a big group of new friends to drink with, party with, and pretend I wasn't grieving with. I kept my mum's death a secret for months, eventually telling a new friend at a house party when he was already drunk. I was so scared of being treated differently that I learned to hide my grief, only crying when I was alone and turning to weed, MDMA, and the drum and bass music scene to drown out the rising tide of emotions that crashed their way through my days. My biggest discovery – that being in another country had apparently granted me the ability to ignore the trauma I'd been through – precipitated my way of life for the next few years.

After my year in San Francisco I began to travel extensively through Asia and South America, writing about my experiences online and establishing a freelance travel writing career as a result. Whenever I felt my grieving mind become more sensitive, more primed, more ready to collapse, I immediately booked another flight, researched another destination, signed up for another volunteering project in a place where I knew nobody and would be challenged every day by its foreign strangeness. Dad and I kept in touch regularly, alternating between Skype calls over crackly webcams in internet cafes, and emails with subject lines saying 'Hello!' in each new country's local language. I did miss him, and I knew he sometimes worried about my safety, but the pull to continue moving was a heady drug.

I really thought I'd discovered the key to getting over grief. It would just fade into the background – all I had to do was ignore it for long enough. It would take seven years for me to realise that by running away from my grief, I was simply putting off the inevitable. Those overwhelming emotions hadn't disappeared by dint of my constant movement. Instead, they were coiled up tight in my chest, waiting for a chance to spring out. It was just a matter of time.

When that grief-collision finally happened in the summer of 2016 I was back in England, living in an East London apartment with two friends and finishing a master's degree in narrative non-fiction. I'd chosen to write a book about Mum's death and my ensuing travels for my masters, thinking that it had been long enough since her death for me to weather any emotional difficulties that might arise. Instead, constantly reliving those events alerted my obstinate mind to the fact that I still hadn't really dealt with the trauma of watching her die.

I began to break down.

Leaving the apartment became increasingly difficult when I couldn't decide what clothes to wear, what to do with my hair, whether I needed water or spare food or an umbrella. If people made eye contact with me in the street I felt acutely uncomfortable, as if their gaze was burning into me. Unbidden thoughts of embarrassment and catastrophe gatecrashed my mind. What if someone attacked me from behind? What if my train was targeted by a terrorist?

A low-level sense of panic began to accompany my daily life, until I eventually realised I was losing grip enough to warrant finding a therapist. She helped to stabilise me somewhat, and I spent a few months talking through the sudden influx of grief-related emotions overwhelming me. I began to feel that I could get through this. What I could never have foreseen was the gradual decline of my dad's health.

In early 2017, Dad was 78 years old. He'd started complaining of shortness of breath less than two years before, and had diligently endured dozens of doctor's appointments and tests until they ascertained that he had idiopathic fibrosis. His lungs were slowly stiffening. There was no cure and it would undoubtedly get worse, but at the time it didn't seem too serious.

But at the end of February, a week before my birthday, Dad called me to say he was finding it hard to breathe. A few days later I picked up the phone and Dad told me he was in hospital. He'd called an ambulance to get there – "I didn't want to worry you, Flor."

My heart broke. I'd spent the last few years alternating between worry about my dad's eventual death, and feeling that nothing bad could possibly happen to him for a very long time. We'd already been through enough, surely?

That week, Dad had a pacemaker fitted and went back to his house. We both tried pretending that things were fine, but by June he was in hospital again, in an even worse condition, and it wasn't long before the doctors said he had just months left to live. "Strangely, I'm not worried about it," Dad said, as we sat together on the sofa in his upstairs bedroom. "Dying just makes me imagine going to sleep, and I'm actually most comfortable when I'm lying down." My reaction was similarly strange, because I barely reacted. This felt like it made sense – of course I'd have to navigate the surreal situation of another parent's death. In hindsight, I realise that numb acceptance was probably shell-shock.

In July I moved out of my East London flat and into my dad's house to care for him. The following few months were the most traumatic I've ever lived through. The relationship between Dad and I was more complex than with my mum: I had inherited both his stubbornness and his sense of pride, so our relationship had always been a little fraught. The tension and pressure of terminal illness heightened every emotion for both of us.

Unlike my mum's death, which was relatively quick and constantly attended by doctors and hospice nurses, my dad's decline was home-based. I was the sole point of contact for every decision which had to be made, and I felt in no way equal to the task.

When Dad knew he was terminal, he thankfully felt able to speak honestly about "the end," and told me early on that he'd like to be at a hospice "when it happened". We contacted the hospice which had looked after Mum, and their staff were incredible from the outset, quickly becoming a key support system for Dad and me during those months. I had regular sessions with a family worker at the hospice who acted as a therapist of sorts, allowing me to talk and cry about how scared and overwhelmed I felt. A lovely palliative care nurse visited Dad every week to assess his condition, and made multiple calls to various council organisations. They delivered a hospital-style bed, oxygen machines, and a commode chair, and even asked if we needed a stairlift fitted. And the biggest provision they made was to tell the council we needed daily visits from a carer. Aisha came twice a day to help Dad with washing, getting changed, eating, and brushing his teeth, and generally fostered the kind of calm, capable demeanour which both Dad and I desperately needed (but were both too proud to actively seek out ourselves). I also made the hospice staff repeatedly promise me that they'd admit Dad to the hospice when I couldn't cope with the emotional burden of caring for him any more – and they were the only professional organisation who really took charge of Dad's illness and lifted the pressure for me.

Dad's ability to move independently decreased each day, but his mind was still as sharp as ever. For someone who'd always been acutely in control of his life, this dependence on others was the cruellest of ironies. He took out his frustrations on me, and we argued a lot. Despite knowing these were the last moments I'd have with my dad I couldn't bear to watch him slowly dying. My emotions had already been at breaking point before his diagnosis, and I simply couldn't deal with the knowledge that soon I'd have to face the harshest wave of fresh grief all over again.

What helped during this time was being honest and vocal about what I was dealing with. I'd only been twenty years old when Mum died – I hadn't yet realised that the ensuing grief and loss was mine to interpret however I saw fit, so I'd done what society seemed to suggest and simply hidden it from public view. I knew no different, and thought that being silent and stoic was the only real option available to me. But with Dad's approaching death I realised just how much I needed the support of other people. I needed an army. Even if they couldn't actually prevent what was happening, I still needed them on my side, ready to help me battle through this.

So I wrote articles about my anticipatory grief on my website. I spoke at length on Instagram Stories about how I was feeling, and I began following grief accounts on Twitter. I messaged my friends constantly. I didn't shy away from explaining how scared and vulnerable and alone I felt about dealing with this. And something shifted. I felt less alone than I had during Mum's death.

My dad died on his 79th birthday, in the hospice he'd been moved to just days before. The same hospice where my mum died, in fact. I wasn't there when it happened; a hospice nurse phoned me just before midnight to tell me. It still feels taboo for me to say this, but I was relieved when Dad died. Not because I wanted it to happen, but because I knew he'd been suffering in a state he absolutely hated. He was a proud man who had excelled at looking after himself, so to have his autonomy taken from him was an indignity I couldn't bear to see. In contrast, I cherish the thought that dying on his birthday was a choice he was still able to make. For a man who had a lifelong love of theatre, it was also wonderfully Shakespearean.

The year of grief which followed my dad's death was undoubtedly the worst year of my life – but it led me to realise how many of us go through this kind of grief. In fact, the last decade of grief has been an education like no other. No matter how much you think you're prepared for a parent's death, it's still impossible to really know what your life will be like without them. It's also impossible to know how you're going to react.

2

The Limbo State of Anticipatory Grief

Anticipatory grief is a surreal experience to navigate. You know there's a death coming, but there's no changing course. It's like standing on a train track watching a train moving ever closer. You're totally impotent. You have to wait for it to come at its own speed until it hits you. And if you've been hit by that train before, you know how much it's going to hurt.

When my mum was given two weeks to live, I went into a state of sudden shock. A fortnight definitely wasn't long enough to absorb the fact that she was unexpectedly dying – and because she'd also suffered a recent stroke, she had virtually no ability to communicate with us anymore. My days were spent journeying to and from hospital, eating microwave meals and canteen sandwiches, desperately willing her to speak to me and trying my hardest not to imagine my life without her in it. But I couldn't stop my mind jumping from my hypothetical wedding day to my hypothetical babies, to every mundane situation in between which I'd always assumed she'd be a part of. Hiding beneath it all was the surreal knowledge that I simply couldn't understand that new future. It couldn't be real.

In comparison, Dad was told he was terminal eight months before his death. When I first found out I was going to watch my second parent die, I made a bizarre attempt at preparation (which was actually more like self-preservation). I'd already spent so many years grieving for Mum that my mind was anxiously impatient to get started on a process I knew would exhaust me in every possible way. I was trying to get a head-start on feeling awful, as if that way I'd perhaps recover more quickly at the other end.

During those months, I wrote in my diary:

This isn't permanent. It can't be. My life exists in another place: even if I've stepped unwillingly away from it for now, I still get to return to it afterwards. My normal, real, loved life – full of travel and spontaneity, friends and photography, chaos and movement, excitement and challenges. Challenges

*I want to embark on, not ones which have been thrust on me
with such force that I feel as if my back might break.*

But truthfully, Dad's illness did feel permanent. I had a
strong sense of foreboding that he might be stuck in
some phase of dying forever – or rather, that the way I
felt during this time would last forever (this fear of a
"limbo state" was so strong, in fact, that I still have
nightmares about it today). I knew his death was going
to shape me into yet another version of myself, in the
same way that Mum's death had completely changed
me as a person. And I was so scared of who that new
version might be.

Looking back now, I can see that I was going
through anticipatory grief. It's not the same as the grief
you feel after someone's died, which is a more static
type of emotional response, and only occurs after the
fact. Anticipatory grief is like being stuck in limbo. You
have to manage your feelings about the future at the
same time as managing the very real and often
constantly-changing present. That present is the person
you love actively dying in front of you. It's a hell of a
lot to take.

Adjusting to someone's terminal diagnosis is not the same as coping with their death

Learning that someone you love is going to die is overwhelming. Your sense of normal transforms in an instant; suddenly you realise that your life is going to change drastically. But a terminal diagnosis can precipitate that change at an incredible speed.

There's the uncertainty of knowing this person's life now has a time limit, but having no idea of how long they might have left. Is it days, weeks, or only hours? Suddenly you start to overanalyse their every moment, their every breath. You harangue the doctors for more details, picking apart their language as if it hides a clue to what they're not telling you. The situation feels never-ending, and sometimes you think you might already be in purgatory. You can't rely on any information: things change all the time and nothing is stable. What you were told yesterday is suddenly no longer the case, and yet you cling to it because you're desperate for any kind of structure to hang all the unexpectedness on.

So you try to find tiny morsels of normality wherever you can. If you can't find them inside the house which now resembles a hospital ward, you decide this "new normal" is totally manageable. Occasionally you catch yourself discussing commodes and bedpans with the visiting carer (who has keys to your house but you still aren't sure you're pronouncing their name correctly), and you studiously ignore that twist in your stomach which shouts, "THIS ISN'T RIGHT!" You pretend and pretend and pretend that you're coping. *This is just a blip*, you tell yourself. *Everything will go back to normal soon. It has to.*

You're always on high alert

Every day, I was desperately trying to envisage how I'd deal with Dad's absence while he was lying there in front of me – his health steadily decreasing, my responsibilities increasing. Every day I had to re-adjust to the things he could no longer do. In every conversation with the carer, the doctor, the hospice worker, the counsellor or any of my friends, I had to re-explain the level he was at now. Every time I spoke to Dad I had to try and parse his emotions, and try my best to match them so I didn't upset him.

I couldn't leave the house unless Dad knew well in advance and felt comfortable with the idea, and unless I'd made sure there would be someone else in the house to help if needed. Spending nights away from the house felt out of the question, but I could never sleep properly at home, either: my ears were always straining for something out of the ordinary. If I went to the toilet I thought he'd suddenly shout for me. When showering, the water would obscure any noises he made. Every tiny sound could be interpreted as the doorbell, or the phone, or a creaking floorboard in his room, or the little handheld bell which he began to ring when his voice grew too weak. Early each morning and late each night, I'd peer through the crack in his door and see him lying with his mouth open. He was so motionless that I had to wait until I heard his ragged breath to know he was still alive.

Living in a constant state of high alert is exhausting. You're always tense, jumping at every noise, primed for the next possible emergency. You're waiting for the inevitable to happen – but you have no idea when that will be. So while your actions and behaviours are being forced to develop, your mind is trying to keep up: learning how to live in this "new normal" moment by moment, while constantly expecting them to die.

Your emotions fluctuate extremely quickly

You might feel as if you're going mad. A sense of isolation can overtake you: you don't want to burden those around you with the awful details, but equally, you can't pretend it isn't happening. So you stop accepting invitations to go out – it's too difficult to arrange the requisite care, anyway – and if you do go anywhere you don't talk much. Instead, you get lost inside your own head.

You begin to resent the situation. *My life was going*

pretty well before all this happened, you think – and now suddenly this diagnosis has ruined every possibility of happiness for a long time to come. If you've experienced intense grief before, you're well aware of how huge the emotional fallout from this will be. You feel a bone-deep urge to scream about how unfair all of this is on you.

And then you feel immensely guilty. *How can I be bitter when they're the one who's dying? How can I be so selfish? So self-involved?* You feel guilty for not doing enough to make their remaining life better. Guilty for not coming up with fun experiences – hell, even fun conversation topics – which might distract them from what's happening. Guilty that your first instinct is to hide away, instead of rolling up your sleeves and becoming an expert in caring for them. What kind of daughter does this make you?

Fury comes from nowhere. It boils up inside and flies out of you at sudden, unexpected moments. Sometimes you throw plates so hard they shatter. Sometimes you shout incomprehensible noises at the hook on the bathroom door when it threatens to break.

Heart-thumping panic arrives out of nowhere, too. Your knees grow weak as you walk down the street, and you find yourself collapsing by a tree in the park when your lungs won't work the way they should. You wonder if *you* might be dying. Can people's bodies give up while they're waiting for someone else to die?

You worry, often, that this is going to damage you much more than you first thought. You're scared that you aren't competent enough to handle all this. You're terrified that this will never end.

If you've felt any of the above emotions, I can only say that in moments of immense difficulty, moments where your life is unrecognisable in the worst of ways, you have to draw strength from wherever you feel able.

Ask for help – even if you feel awkward

During the last months of my dad's life, I felt as if I was on duty 24/7. All the people who were there to help me (the nurse, hospice worker, carer and my community of friends) felt like drops in an ocean I had to navigate alone. My dad wanted more from me than I could physically and emotionally offer. If I said good morning at 10 a.m. (when he'd been sleeping until that time – I knew because I'd put my head around the door several times that morning) he'd chastise me for 'abandoning' him and not saying hello earlier. I couldn't win. He was fighting a battle much bigger than the two of us, so he took it out on me: because I was his only remaining family, because he trusted me, and simply because I was there. It didn't change how overwhelmed I felt, though.

If someone hasn't died yet, you somehow feel less deserving of help. It's human nature to downplay the severity of a situation like this because we don't want it to be so severe. It's also really problematic. I was desperate for someone else to take the reins and handle just a bit of the responsibility – but I also wanted to take it all on myself, as I felt like it was my job. That contradiction almost stopped me from reaching out when I really needed help.

Luckily, before it got too bad I made a WhatsApp group with my closest friends called "Flora is going to be OK". They dutifully posted daily affirmations, gifs of kittens and messages of love and support to buoy me up. The group also doubled as a place for me to share crucial information about Dad's condition, without having to explain myself multiple times in separate conversations.

Be aware of hospice care – positives and negatives

There are various avenues of professional support available when someone is dying. They can also help you with the strange subject of *where* someone might be when they die.

I only knew about the possibilities of hospice care

because Mum had been referred there by her hospital doctors. It was a blessing in disguise: because we'd already experienced the calm and comforting nature of the hospice, Dad decided early on that he'd like to die there instead of at home. I also think he'd considered that dying at home would make it difficult for me to live there afterwards.

The big downside to the hospice was something I only discovered when it was already happening: hospice care isn't usually a long-term option. Because hospices are usually charity-run, they don't have the funds or capacity to admit someone unless they're in the "final stages of life." As you'd expect, this is something of a debatable timeframe! When I pushed for a real answer, the hospice staff admitted it would be when Dad had around two weeks to live. So although we all knew he'd go to the hospice at some point, it was almost impossible to predict when. Meanwhile, I was becoming more and more unravelled – and when Dad's health and my sanity eventually reached a crisis point, the hospice agreed to admit him for respite care. I had to lie, telling my dad he was moving there for good; he was so weak that I knew the thought of going to the hospice, then returning to the house, then eventually returning to the hospice again to die, would be too much for him.

After an ambulance ride to the hospice and while

Dad settled into his room, the doctors and I talked. We all agreed that he couldn't move back home – but he also couldn't spend more than a week at the hospice because he wasn't at the "final stage." My heart sank as the doctor told me I'd have to research nursing homes: the ones which I could travel to easily, which had good food on offer, and which were within my budget.

I wanted to scream. I'd thought that once I got him to the hospice, I could finally be his daughter again, instead of his carer – and now I had to find an appropriate nursing home for an undefinable amount of time? When we finally told Dad this information, he visibly weakened. I knew that mentally he couldn't cope with a move to another new location, and I was right. Dad died only a few days later, sooner than the hospice staff anticipated.

Forgive yourself

If you're not professionally trained as a carer, then caring for the terminally ill is not your job. My dad was insistent that we could cope with his decline together, just the two of us, because I think it helped him to pretend things weren't as serious as they actually were. This pretence did nothing to help me. I felt terrified and overwhelmed. There were so many logistical aspects I simply wasn't capable of handling. What if he fell and I couldn't get him up? What if he died in the night and I found his body the next morning?

When I told Dad we needed to accept the hospice's offer of a daily carer, I felt I was failing him. It brought a lot of guilt – surely I should *want* to care for him? Surely I should be enough? More than anything, though, I wanted to be his daughter instead of a totally untrained ad-hoc nurse. Which meant I had to forgive myself for not being a perfect human who could handle all aspects of this alone.

There's a big difference between nursing a parent through a bout of flu and caring for them as they die. In place of the near-certainty that they'll get better and things will return to normal, you're faced with a stark awareness that there's only one outcome. Of course, it's still not easy to hand over care responsibilities to someone else. You often feel obliged to do more than you're able, pushing yourself too hard in an effort to be the only help they need. But you have to forgive yourself for not doing the things you think that you "should" do in this period. Forgive yourself for resentment and guilt and any other 'bad' feelings you're having towards the person. They know this is hard for you, too. Sometimes you have no ability to do anything except let the time unwind. And that's OK.

Make space for yourself and take time out to

recharge

Finding pockets of time where you can sink back into your old, comfortable normal will keep you sane. For me, it was either walking the streets around my house or going for a run. The latter was a new hobby but Dad saw the benefit in it – and if I knew I had half an hour where he wasn't expecting me to be at home, I felt a little less pressured. Being outside and getting the frantic energy out of my body was cathartic, and helped me to process what I was feeling at my own pace.

If there wasn't a chance to carve out half an hour of privacy, I had other fail-safe distractions from my panic. The Candy Crush game became my absolute godsend! When I felt my stress levels rising, I grabbed my phone and either hid in the bathroom or on my sofa bed in the living room. Playing that vapid, mindless phone game, full of colours and simple yet engrossing actions, made my logical brain kick into gear. It brought me out of my over-thinking state and pulled me away from the panic-attack ledge.

And when I remembered, I closed my eyes and listened to a meditation on the Headspace app. My mind was so cluttered and tense all the time that I barely even noticed how much I was fearfully projecting into the future, but meditation made me focus on the immediate present. It didn't necessarily last that long, but for a little while, I could loosen the hold that pre-grief had over me and just put one foot in front of the other.

Ready yourself for other people's false hope

Watching the people you love get sick is always difficult. But when you know they won't get better, it becomes frustrating and painful to hear false positivity from people who simply don't understand the gravity of the situation.

"I hope he's on the mend soon!"

"We're sending lots of get-well wishes!"

"I'm sure he'll be fine!"

Nope. He's dying. My dad is definitely, diagnosably, dying. When it was happening I had to say this to myself, because I needed time to adjust to the idea. I had to prepare myself as much as possible for what was inevitable – and yet I couldn't directly say it out loud, because it was so horrible and unexpected and so hilariously awkward. And I couldn't bear it when someone seemed to think death didn't happen in general, and certainly wouldn't happen to him.

Don't pin your hopes on any deathbed revelations

Most of us have extremely complex relationships with our parents. There's a frustratingly inaccurate assumption perpetuated by Hollywood that someone's deathbed is where they want to clear the air of any bad blood – but in reality, a lot of dying people want to pretend as hard as possible that nothing serious is really happening. That extends to their last words and final apologies and everything else.

Try not to feel guilty if there are issues which don't get resolved, or conversations which are left unsaid. I wanted to clear the air with my dad about years of simmering tension between us, but although there were plenty of moments when I *could* have said something, ultimately the framing of our relationship simply didn't allow for it.

How to prepare for their death together

A dying person's emotional landscape is highly changeable. The psychiatrist Elisabeth Kübler-Ross wrote famously about the five stages of grief – denial, anger, bargaining, depression, and acceptance – which a dying person will go through. My dad's denial was heartbreaking to watch. He ordered a diary for the next calendar year. He scoffed at people's overtly emotional cards and emails, saying "It's not like I'm dying tomorrow!" when he definitely could have.

But the anger was worse. Dad's explosive reactions were directed at me because I was the safest option – someone who wouldn't leave him. I tried my best not to take it personally; Dad was such a proud man that I knew he couldn't show his fear to his doctors, his carers, or even his friends. I knew it was an anger borne of fear and confusion about his life coming to an end, but that didn't make it hurt any less. As a result, I cherished the moments where Dad was in a good enough mood for us to behave relatively normally, like we had before his terminal diagnosis. These were the times that I tried to remember more vividly, and this is how I did it.

Talk to them

Ask questions about things. Ask about their family, stories from their childhood. Reconfirm the things you half-remember. Make notes (although maybe not in front of them). It's amazing how quickly you can forget details when there's nobody alive to confirm them. You'll be grateful for this later.

Write things down

Throughout Mum's death, I kept track of what was happening: a continuous Word document stayed open on my laptop. I didn't do this purposefully at all, but I had a strong sense that I needed to preserve the thoughts and emotions I was feeling at the time. I did the same with Dad, although it was a much more conscious decision by then. Writing has become my space to process my thoughts, so I knew it would help me better understand and confront what was happening. Now, when I look back at those notes, I see the person I was and the positive developments I've made since. It's also reminded me of many details – like the little phrases Dad said which I might otherwise have forgotten. I highly recommend writing through your grief, whether it's anticipatory or after the event.

Make voice recordings

When Mum died, I kept listening to an answerphone message she left for me in the hospital. After a few weeks, it was auto-deleted from my phone – and I realised how vulnerable my sensory memories of her were. So in Dad's last months I often left my phone recorder app running while we chatted. I sometimes felt a bit sneaky doing this, but I knew I'd probably be thankful in the long run. It's been two years and I still haven't found the courage to listen to them yet, but at least I know they're there (and on an external hard drive, and backed up on Dropbox too).

Take photos

Perhaps it's because I knew I was making so many voice recordings and written notes, but I wasn't keen on taking photos of Dad in his last months – though I do have a few of him in hospital because he wanted to see how he looked with a month of beard growth, something he'd never willingly have chosen! But many people find immense comfort in photos. Take photos if that feels like a good thing to do – many people have photos of their own hand holding their loved one's hand. I didn't do this, but I treasure a couple of quick phone photos of my dad.

Look through old photos together

We spent a few afternoons looking through some of Dad's old photo albums while he told me stories about his early life. I tried hard not to put too much pressure on him, but I was acutely aware that this would be the final chance I'd have to know these details.

Respect their conversation topics – but if you can, talk about their final wishes

Understandably, many people want to ignore the fact that they're dying. If that's the case, just be there. Listen to them. Watch TV with them. Make sure they know you're around and willing to be with them despite the situation.

But if they're happy to talk about death, it's really valuable to ask them some questions – particularly if the imminent death is of your last/only parent, as you could well be responsible for organising their affairs.

Thankfully my dad was a very pragmatic man, and as soon we knew his illness was terminal, Dad instructed me to grab an empty notebook and start writing. Together we worked through all the information I'd need to handle his death. Looking back now, it was such a brave thing to do – and yet totally in line with the person he was. Over the next eighteen months, I noted down everything which needed to be sorted out concerning his death in that little blue notebook – and it turned out to be a very good idea. Why? Because in the first few months of grief, you start forgetting absolutely everything. And there's always something else to do: a phone call from a company you forgot he had an account with, or an art gallery expecting a new annual subscription.

I now refer to all the information we wrote down as "death admin" – and the next chapter details every stage of that process.

3

Death Admin

The morning after my dad's death, I called the hospice. To ask them... what? To re-confirm that he'd died? I didn't know what else to do. I guess I wanted to make sure that I hadn't been forgotten about. The experience of the last few months had been so intense and overwhelming that I couldn't conceive it was just – OVER.

Of course, it's not over at all; there's just a different set of challenges to face. With the blurry, decade-old details of my mum's death in my mind, I had words and phrases on the tip of my tongue – death registration, certificate, funeral directors, probate – but I didn't know what was most important, or what needed to be dealt with first.

I felt very much like a child playing with a grown-up topic she didn't understand.

Thankfully I'd had time over the past months to research what the process of dealing with someone's death looked like, but I was still overwhelmed by how many bureaucratic boxes needed to be ticked. Just because you've done the research, that doesn't mean you're prepared to actually do it all. And it doesn't help that the process of death admin is long, serious, scarily official and all takes place while you're extremely emotional.

My dad died on a Friday night, so there was no doctor available to officially confirm his death until the Monday morning. That gave me some time to absorb what had happened in my own space. I spent Saturday scouring the internet for help with probate, with funeral directors, with death registrations, with finances. I still felt numb. My logical brain had piped up, trying to take control of something – and writing out a list of requisite tasks made the most sense.

Viewing his body and getting the doctor's medical certificate

By Monday I'd decided that I did want to see Dad's body. I hadn't done this with my mum - I'd been present at her death so it hadn't felt necessary. But I hadn't been there when Dad died. People always talk about 'getting closure' and I didn't know if I'd automatically got that from seeing Mum, so after struggling with the decision for a while, I eventually decided that I might regret it if I didn't say goodbye to Dad's physical form.

My boyfriend drove us to the hospice and Mum's best friend met us there. Together, we went inside and were led down a flight of stairs to a chilly corridor. The nurse told me that he looked very peaceful, but also that he was very cold. I went in alone. He didn't look like my dad anymore. His skin was extremely cold and firm, and I couldn't do more than touch his hand. Looking at his impossibly still form, I wondered if I'd regret my decision. What if this was how I'd remember him from now on? What if I couldn't shake this image from my mind?

After the viewing was over, a hospice worker led me to a cosy little room with a jug of water and a vase of flowers on a table. She gave me a collection of my dad's belongings in his black bag, which had a brown paper label with his name on strung around the strap, and an assortment of carrier bags. She also handed me the official medical certificate from the doctor which showed the cause of death. It felt absurdly casual to be handed Dad's final possessions like this, but at least the first official task was complete.

Registering the death

The next task I had to face was officially registering
Dad's death. I headed for the local registry office armed
with everything that could possibly be relevant: Dad's
birth certificate, driving licence, passport, and the
medical certificate from the doctor saying he'd died.

Registering a death is a surreal experience. We sat
in a waiting room used for registering births,
marriages, and deaths, and I tried not to see the new
parents rocking their tiny babies or the loved-up
couples gazing happily at each other in nearby seats. I
tried to ignore the brochures for honeymoon
destinations scattered on the tables and clutched the
plastic binder filled with Dad's documents. I had a
strong urge to shout out my reason for being there.

When our number was called, we were led into a
little office covered in cat decorations, where a
somewhat stern woman took me through the process
of registering Dad's death. I filled out some forms,
showed her Dad's documents, and in return she gave
me his official death certificate (along with five copies,
which I paid extra for), a 'Registration and Notification
of Death' on a single sheet of white paper, and a
'Certificate for Cremation' on green paper. I couldn't
quite believe how formal this whole process was. More
pressingly, it was hard to stop myself from making

jokes about her office decor choices. Dad would've loved the excessive cat paraphernalia.

When I got home later that afternoon, I made a few photocopies of the death certificate on the off-chance that some organisations would happily take a copy instead of the real thing. I also started the gruelling process of phoning the requisite "official" people: Dad's registered doctor to tell them that he'd died; the oxygen suppliers to pick up their machines from the house; the medical company who'd provided Dad with a hospital bed, who said they'd collect it in a week – which ended up being the day before the funeral. Every completed task was ticked off my already alarmingly long list, and the dates of arranged pickups were jotted down too. I didn't want any surprise visitors.

Choosing a funeral home and discussing the funeral

Planning the funeral was the part I'd dreaded most. In theory, I should have researched a few different funeral homes, but I simply didn't have the capacity to think about comparing costs and services. I just wanted to get it over with, so I went with a friend's recommendation.

At the funeral home, I sat beside my mum's best

friend (as my surrogate mum, she was my designated funeral-planning companion), at a round table in a stuffy room with no windows. Opposite me was a woman in a charcoal-grey suit with her hair scraped back; between us was my phone, recording our conversation on a voice note app. Recording all these administrative meetings was perhaps my best idea throughout this first week of grief, as I really wasn't absorbing what anyone said to me. Instead, I stared down at a glossy brochure divided into neat little squares, each containing different styles of coffins at different prices. The full enormity of what I was doing kept hitting me like a sucker punch, and it was hard to focus.

First, we talked about where and when the funeral would be held. I was pretty sure Dad would have wanted a funeral at the same church where Mum's service had been held. Our family wasn't particularly religious, but we had social connections to that church, so it was an easy decision (and my mum's best friend also knew the vicar well).

Once we'd agreed on a provisional date for the funeral, the funeral director made a few calls to confirm that the date was suitable for both the church and the crematorium. Dad had told me in his last months that he'd prefer a cremation over a burial. I'd found my mum's burial pretty traumatic and had collapsed beside the grave as her coffin was lowered into it, so I think he wanted to spare me the possibility of experiencing that a second time. As the main service would take place at the church, the crematorium only needed to be booked for a committal instead of the half-hour service they could have offered.

Eventually, it was confirmed that the funeral would be held on 9 November, almost three weeks after Dad's death. I didn't want to think about where his body would be throughout that time, but I did feel relieved that we'd made a concrete decision.

Unfortunately, that relief didn't last long. The next topic was the cost of all these funeral arrangements, and it was shocking. I hadn't even thought about money amidst Mum's death as my dad had thankfully never mentioned it, although after he died I found the paperwork documenting the cost of Mum's graveyard plot and headstone carving.

Once the charcoal-grey woman had told me about fees for the coffin, the cremation, the two doctors who have to sign the death certificate, and the funeral home's services, the grand total came to £4,500. Thankfully I knew my dad's savings would cover it – although I still had to successfully navigate accessing that money at his bank.

Arranging the funeral service

We must have booked an appointment with the vicar, but I don't remember doing it. All I remember is sitting in a little room attached to the church while the vicar and my mum's best friend discussed everything we needed to arrange for Dad's funeral service.

Similar to the funeral home, there was an alarming amount of planning involved. What songs and hymns would Dad have wanted? Who would give the eulogy? What readings would there be, and who would give them? How on earth do you decide what music plays while your dad's coffin enters and leaves a church?

Both my parents loved classical music, and I had vague memories of how perfect the music at Mum's funeral had been, but suddenly that part of my mind was empty. Under pressure, I felt unable to choose The Right Song to send Dad off. I spent one fruitless afternoon searching through drawers for Mum's funeral program, thinking we might have printed our music choices inside, but I never found it.

The vicar was gentle and understanding, but I still felt overwhelmed by responsibility. I knew I wanted to give the eulogy for Dad, just like I'd done for Mum, but I was at a loss for music and readings. Eventually, I asked two of Dad's closest friends if they'd be happy to each choose and deliver a reading, and I asked Mum's church-going friend to give me a list of five funeral-appropriate hymns and then I chose my three favourites.

Organising the wake

Once the funeral arrangements had been made, I visited a lovely pub near the church to see if they could host the wake. The manager was an absolute dream. Once I'd asked about hosting a wake there on our chosen date, he immediately brought out a food list and suggested possible combinations for a funeral party. "We could do it in two waves, so the second set of food gets brought out when the crematorium guests arrive," he said, and I could have hugged him.

The wake cost me £200 for renting the space and providing food, and was in no way as complicated as the funeral home had been. Thank goodness.

Closing Dad's accounts and redirecting his regular payments

My dad had accounts with three different banks. I phoned them all first, asked to be transferred to their bereavement department, explained the situation, asked to book an appointment with a nearby branch, and then finally went to visit in person. Tightly clutching my plastic folder of documents – Dad's death certificate, his will, his bank cards, the funeral invoice, and my ID – I sat in the windowless offices of each bank and successfully organised Dad's finances.

Dad made me sole executor in the final months of his life, and although I was grateful I didn't have to co-ordinate these appointments with someone else, it was still an exhausting list to take full responsibility for. At those meetings, Dad's bank accounts were closed and the money in them was re-deposited into my accounts. Because I planned to continue living in his house, I re-directed the direct debits which I still needed (mainly utility bills, internet, and council tax) to come out of my accounts instead, and finally asked the bank to print out 'date of death' bank balances, which I'd eventually use for probate purposes.

Sharing news of his death

Dad's death wasn't a shock. Most of his friends and mine already knew it was going to happen. We'd had months to come to terms with Dad's diagnosis; months where the information moved through different communities and those who wanted to visit him in hospital had done so. Thankfully, this meant telling people about his actual death wasn't too upsetting.

In comparison, sharing the news of my mum's sudden and unexpected death was difficult. Outside my family's closest friends, not many people knew she'd even been ill. Dad had to pick up the phone and explain to a shocked number of people that Mum had died. Occasionally I answered the house phone and found myself comforting someone who'd only just heard. It was a jarring experience.

Unexpected issues before the funeral

It was similarly jarring to lose confidence in the people responsible for handling my dad's funeral. A week before it was due to take place, I spent a tearful afternoon looking through Dad's wardrobe and agonising over what clothes he should be dressed in. The depressed part of me felt like this was redundant – he was going to be cremated, after all – but I couldn't quite contemplate any other alternative. Was he still in his pyjamas, wherever he was?

Once I'd chosen an outfit, I put everything into a bag and headed for the funeral home. I'd assumed I could just hand the clothes over and leave, but the receptionist clearly thought differently. She didn't ask for Dad's name or mine; instead, she held a pen poised over a notepad, apparently waiting to write down an itemised list of the clothes I'd brought. I had no idea I was expected to do this, and it was a shocking surprise.

Earlier that day, I'd also had a voicemail from the

funeral director. She couldn't get in touch with the church to confirm the funeral and seemed to think I would have better luck contacting them. Not only was this an odd assumption which she had no grounds to make, but her panicked tone had also sent me spiralling. Now, confronted by a second problem at the funeral home, I didn't feel at all confident that Dad's funeral was going to go smoothly. The enormity of the last weeks and months pressed in on me and I started to cry, which only made me feel more upset! Thankfully, once I began to explain my worries, I was ushered off to a back room where a second funeral director told me she'd be taking care of Dad's service instead.

But unfortunately, the problems continued. The day before Dad's funeral, I had a call from the funeral home to remind me that I hadn't ordered any flowers for the service. "At this point, there won't be any flowers in the church at all," she told me. I was stunned. The mental image of a bare coffin with no flowers surrounding it was unbearably sad, but planning for this detail hadn't even crossed my mind. The woman on the phone explained that a nearby florist could provide a flower arrangement and they'd add it to my funeral invoice.

The funeral

Both my parents' funerals were held at the same church. I had the strangest sense of déjà vu as I walked past rows of seated people and up the central aisle for the second time in a decade. But there were some crucial differences between Mum's funeral and Dad's, and oddly enough, I was able to learn from previous experience.

At Mum's funeral, I stood at the church's front doors with my dad to greet people as they arrived. It was awkward and emotional: some people clearly recognised me, though I didn't know them, and others wanted hugs or conversations which I didn't feel comfortable having. For my dad's funeral, I made it much easier on myself: I arrived at the church just before the service started, slipping through the doors and walking straight up the aisle to my reserved seat at the front.

When I saw Mum's coffin enter through the church doors, I felt a visceral reaction to seeing it move. My first instinct was to turn my face away and squeeze my boyfriend's hand until he indicated that that part was over. Eight years later my instinct was the same at Dad's funeral: I felt strongly that seeing the coffin in motion would be too much for me, so I asked the funeral director ahead of time for Dad's coffin to be at the front of the church before I arrived.

During Mum's funeral, my front-row seat was

somehow on the opposite side of the church to the lectern, where I had to stand to deliver the eulogy. This meant I had to walk directly in front of her coffin – something I spent the first ten minutes of the funeral panicking about. However, that experience was strangely helpful when arranging my Dad's funeral with the vicar, as I actively requested to sit as close to the lectern as possible.

Giving the eulogy

I gave the eulogy at both my parents' funerals. Though it was an emotional experience each time, it was still an easy decision for me. Being the daughter of two theatre professionals means I'm pretty confident in public speaking, and writing is my cathartic process.

In order to write Dad's eulogy, I began taking notes on my phone about a week before the funeral. Whenever a thought struck me, I added little sentences and ideas, and when I eventually sat down to write, I also dug out Mum's eulogy and used it as a pseudo-template. Once I had a draft, I read it out loud to myself and even practised in the mirror to take the fear out of speaking at the funeral. Then I printed a copy, made pencilled notes of the paragraphs where I wanted to pause for breath (or for the possibility of crying), and slipped the pages into my handbag.

Standing at the lectern, just metres away from my dad's coffin, and looking out at the faces of so many people who loved my whole family, was honestly rather beautiful. I knew how much they missed my parents and how much they wanted to support me. It may sound strange, but if you can have a favourite moment of a funeral, I think giving both these eulogies were mine.

The burial

My mum was buried in a graveyard close to my family home. Dad and I drove there in near silence, parking just outside the gates while I fumbled with the buckle of my black heels and pulled on thicker boots. It was January and it was raining. My dad, ever the forward-thinker, had suggested I bring different shoes so my feet didn't sink into the mud.

When we saw the hearse arrive, we clambered out of our car and joined a sombre procession of people walking behind. The burial was probably the most surreal part of the day, and I didn't handle it all that well. I don't remember much, but friends told me later that as the vicar spoke those famous committal words, I collapsed onto the ground and started sobbing. In hindsight, I'm rather glad I don't remember it.

At the crematorium

My dad's cremation ceremony was much less traumatic. I'd never been inside a crematorium before, so I was understandably nervous about what it would entail. More than anything, I couldn't bear the idea of seeing his coffin vanish behind red velvet curtains (thanks for that image, Hollywood). Of course, I hadn't realised that I'd be allowed to actively voice my concerns. All it took was one conversation with the funeral director, who immediately said she'd ask the congregation to leave the room before Dad's coffin moved at all.

Only a select few people had come from the church to the crematorium – most guests had simply gone straight to the wake. I had my closest friends and boyfriend with me, my dad's closest friends and a few others. Once everyone had arrived I walked in last, just like I'd done at the church, so the coffin was already sitting in the middle of the room, surrounded by flowers. We sang a few hymns and the vicar gave a short speech, and then it was over.

As I walked out of the crematorium, the funeral director handed me a little spray of flowers. "These are from your dad's tributes on his coffin," she said kindly. I almost started crying right there – but out of gratitude, not sadness.

At the wake

I was happily surprised by how much I enjoyed my dad's wake. It was a crisp, bright autumn day; the pub was light and airy, with tables full of delicious food; and so many people I loved were sharing stories about my dad with each other. I left after a few hours in a surreal state of gratitude (and with a platter of leftover sandwiches).

It was miles better than the memories of my mum's wake. After my graveside breakdown, all I'd wanted to do was go home and be alone. So spending a few hours in the back room of a local pub, crammed amongst people who all wanted to tell me how sorry they were for my loss, was not particularly enjoyable. Nor was the man who told me he'd loved my eulogy, and asked if he could get a copy for his children to use as a template when their mum's approaching death took place.

Applying for probate

Probate was the part of death admin that loomed over me the most. I knew the process would take months to complete, and I was worried from a personal standpoint too. Acquiring a Grant of Probate would

give me the legal right to distribute my dad's estate –
but it also meant potentially paying inheritance tax
(IHT) on the estate's value. I was living in Dad's house
and had no plans to move, so the possibility of needing
to sell his house in order to pay off the inheritance tax
was really disconcerting.

So I did what any twenty-nine-year-old bereaved
person does. I buried my head in the sand for a while.
But eventually, the anxiety gnawed away at me so
much that I begrudgingly began researching what to
do. There are two main options for probate in the UK:
completing it yourself by filling out the requisite forms
or hiring a solicitor to do it for you. I spent months
imagining I'd do the forms, but then I actually forced
myself to look through the printed copies from the
government's website. That same day, I started
researching probate solicitors.

Once I decided to hire someone, the process moved
more fluidly. I spoke to a handful of solicitors on the
phone, made lots of notes about their individual offers
and their quoted prices, and chose a firm who charged
a reasonable rate. I turned up at their offices with my
plastic document folder and, most crucially, Dad's will.
They seemed a little surprised to see me in person, but
I didn't want to send such important documents in the
post.

Two months and a few back-and-forth emails later,

the solicitors called to say probate had successfully been granted, and I didn't have to pay any inheritance tax. I settled their invoice and breathed a sigh of relief. As far as I could tell, the admin stage of grief was over.

4

The Little Blue Book

If you're the only person coping with death admin, there's a lot you're suddenly responsible for. You have to piece together a litany of official tasks, often in a specific order, and within a tight timeframe. You've never heard of some processes, and don't know how they work, so you have to learn on the go. Meanwhile, grief is clouding your mind and your capabilities, making it hard to concentrate on any of it.

It took me more than eighteen months to wade through all the admin surrounding Dad's death. I held my breath almost constantly throughout, worrying that something would go wrong. Now, when I flick through the pages of my Little Blue Book, I see scrawled sentences, heavy-handed circles, and question marks littering every page. So much of these

admin tasks could only be completed by other people –
solicitors, funeral directors, bank workers. I simply
had to trust in their capabilities, but it left me
constantly anxious. I'd also become uncomfortably
aware of the "grief fog". After dozens of meetings and
phone calls, only the haziest of details remained in my
mind.

The only thing that kept me feeling somewhat in
control? Writing absolutely everything down. Keeping
lists meant I could track the progression of admin
tasks, and being able to tick them off when they were
finally complete gave me a much-needed rush of
reassurance.

To make it easier for you, this chapter contains
everything you need to do when someone dies. It's an
extensive list of the questions I asked, the documents I
needed, the order I did things in, and the best ways I
could find to minimise the emotional impact of the
whole weird experience of death admin. In honour of
my dad's commendable forward-thinking, it's called
The Little Blue Book.

Write everything down in a notebook

Things will keep coming. You *will* forget what you've
done. Keeping track of dates and meetings and the
admin you've still got to do is a tough job, especially

when your mind is full of grief. Let the book handle it.

Record your conversations

You'll forget a lot of this stuff, but you might also zone out mid-conversation if things are getting too much. Download a voice notes app on your phone – there are plenty of free ones to choose from – and you can listen back later to details you've forgotten. Maybe back them up externally too, on Dropbox or something similar.

Ask for help

Find someone to go with you to the funeral home, to the church to plan the service, to the graveyard, and to the bank. It's great to have some emotional support – but it's also for a logical reason. Two people keeping track of the information is much better than one, particularly because grief is a great memory zapper.

Keep your documents in one place

There's an upsetting amount of official paperwork which you can't lose. I suggest coupling your death admin notebook with a plastic envelope or wallet to keep all your various bits of paper together.

The word 'bereavement' goes a long way

It cuts through long wait times with automated voices on phone calls. It gets you immediate in-person appointments at banks in little private rooms. It snaps people to attention and reminds them they've all had sensitivity training at work. If there's ever a time to pull on their heartstrings, it's now. You're allowed.

Questions to ask before a death

If you can, get this information before they die:
- Where is their will?
- Where are the deeds to their house?
- Where are the registration certificates for their car?
- What are their log-in details and passwords for bank accounts, utility companies, email accounts or similar?
- What is their national insurance number?
- Where are their important documents? These include their birth certificate, marriage certificate, driving licence, and passport.
- What direct debits currently come out of their accounts?
- What utility companies do they use (water, gas, electricity)?

- What other regular bills do they pay (phone bill, internet provider, TV packages)?

Extra questions to cover:
- Do they have any stocks, shares, or bonds?
- Do they have a private pension or life insurance?
- Do they have any sort of funeral plan or 'death in service' benefit?
- Do they have an accountant who's done their taxes in the past? If not, you'll have to file their taxes for the last year they were alive.
- Do they pay memberships or subscriptions to any organisations (art galleries, museums, political parties)?
- Do they make any regular donations to charities?

Don't worry if you can't get answers to all of these questions. The most important one is the location of their will, if they have one. Everything else can be sorted out with the organisations in question – it just might take a little longer.

If they feel comfortable answering, it'll help you emotionally to ask the following questions about their funeral arrangements:
- Do they have any thoughts about their funeral

(songs, music, readings)?

- What sort of flowers would they like at the service?
- Is there anyone who wouldn't be welcome at a funeral?
- What songs would they like to be played? Who would they like to speak? Are there any favourite poems or passages they'd like to be read out?
- Would they like a religious service or not? Do they want any kind of service at all?
- Would they like people to make a donation to a charity of their choice?
- Would they like a newspaper announcement about their death?
- Would they prefer to be buried or cremated?
- Where would they like to be buried? Under a shady tree, in full sunlight, with a gorgeous view, beside another grave? With any possessions? Wedding ring, photos, diaries, a particular object?
- What would they like written on their headstone, if they are having one?
- Where would they like their ashes scattered? At sea, on a hill, in a favourite location, on a grave, buried in a significant place, in an urn on the mantelpiece?

Just after they've died

The first few days of grief are a very odd place to be. It feels as if someone has shaken your emotions up like a snow globe, and nothing has settled yet. Frustratingly, you're also expected to arrange and cancel and explain and pay for several tasks at the same time.

In the first week or so, you'll need to accomplish the following:
- Register the death
- Choose a funeral director / undertaker
- Arrange the funeral
- Organise the wake / funeral reception
- Cancel their bank accounts and divert their direct debits
- Tell people they've died

All these activities will feel totally surreal. That's OK, because they are. If you're struggling with the thought of it all, bear the following in mind:

Your emotions will be all over the place during this period. Accept that you're going to feel overwhelmed and distraught. And numb. And in shock. And unbearably sad. And strangely OK. And utterly confused. All these emotions are completely valid – as is the random order they might appear in.

Try to do only one "big" task each day (and space things out). Although it feels like there is a never-ending list of things to be done, they can be divided into two categories: things you *should* do, which can be put off for longer than you'd think, and things you *have* to do, which are legally and emotionally necessary to sort as quickly as possible, so that you can relax a little.

Remember that you only have to do each of these things once. However uncomfortable, upsetting, inappropriate, or downright ridiculous they might feel, once you've soldiered your way through, they're over and done with.

Getting a medical certificate from the doctor

This medical certificate is the first official evidence that they've died, and will be given to you either by a hospital/hospice doctor, or your local GP. Keep this safe, as you'll need to take it when you're registering the death.

Registering the death

In the UK, a death has to be registered within five

days. You can do this at any registry office, but visiting the one closest to where the person died means you'll get the required documents that same day. Remember to take as many of their personal documents as you can find, as this makes the process easier. You can check online for what your government requires, but it will probably include:

- Birth certificate
- Council tax bill
- Driving licence
- Marriage certificate
- Passport
- Proof of address (i.e. a utility bill)

In return for showing some documents and filling out some forms, you'll be given the following:

- A death certificate and any additional copies
- A Certificate for Burial or Cremation
- A Registration and Notification of Death

It's sensible to buy a few extra death certificates as various banks and other organisations want originals, not copies – I bought five extras at £4 each and that was enough for me. Nevertheless, err on the side of caution here as you don't want to go back to the registry office later. If you think you'll need more, buy them now!

Do you want to see them for a final time?

Open casket funerals aren't that common in the UK so I had to decide whether I wanted to see my dad's body. Generally speaking, if you were present for their death then you may not feel it's necessary to see them again, but it's a completely personal decision.

Choosing a funeral home and funeral director

I know it seems surreal to meet with different funeral directors but I chose the first place I visited and somewhat regret that decision. The people who looked after my dad's funeral really were good at their jobs, but their client-facing skills left a lot to be desired!

Consider doing the following:

○ Research the prices and services of different funeral homes in your area – this can be done online or via phone. You don't have to visit in person at this stage (unless you want to).
○ Bring someone with you to the funeral home for support.
○ Think about whether you get on with the person you're speaking to. You'll be entrusting them with a pretty crucial emotional and logistical task, so you want to feel like you can trust them.

- Ask for quotes before making a decision, as costs can vary significantly between funeral homes.

Most people don't know how expensive a funeral can be until they're in the midst of having to plan one. The cost of a typical funeral in the UK could look like this:

- Coffin price: anywhere from £300 to £3,000
- Fee for the person conducting the funeral: £200
- Cremation fees: £730 (these vary wildly depending on location. A burial costs more, plus there's the eventual cost of a headstone too).
- Two doctors: £160 (this fee is for signing the death certificate and cremation form).
- The funeral home's services: £3500 (includes collection and care of the deceased, and transportation to the funeral).

In total, I spent over £4,500 on my dad's funeral. I don't know how much my mum's funeral cost.

If you're worried about how to pay for a funeral, remember that you're able to use money from their bank or building society account. Most funeral homes need a deposit to secure the funeral date, but the total can be paid later on. You can take the remaining invoice to the bank where they'll pay the remainder out of the deceased person's bank accounts. You can also ask the funeral home about their instalment plan for payments.

Topics you'll discuss at the funeral home:
- What kind of coffin?
- Burial or cremation? If this isn't written in their will then it's up to you to decide. From a purely logical standpoint, a cremation is the less expensive option. A burial requires purchasing a plot, and a headstone later down the line.
- Where will the funeral be held? In a church, outdoors etc?
- What kinds of flowers? Will you arrange this or will the funeral home do it?
- What will they be wearing in the coffin? You can bring a set of their clothes to the funeral home.
- Is there anything else you want in the coffin with them?

Organising the funeral

If you choose to hold the funeral in a church, you'll also need to arrange details with the person conducting it (for me, it was a church vicar). Typical funeral service admin includes:

- Opening music as people arrive, and/or as the coffin arrives.
- Closing music as the coffin leaves, and/or as people leave.
- 3-5 songs or hymns to sing.
- Are you giving a eulogy? If not, who is?
- Will there be any other readings? Are the people giving them choosing what they'll read, or are you?
- A few photos of your parent for the programme (usually for the front and back cover).

Deciding on a date for the funeral

The funeral director usually acts as middleman, ascertaining a date when the funeral service space and the burial/cremation ground (for the committal) are both available. This can feel a little complicated, but all you have to do is suggest possible dates. The funeral director will make the necessary phone calls.

Arranging a wake

In the UK, funerals are often followed by a more informal gathering called a wake. This can be held anywhere, but the most popular options seem to be church halls, pub function rooms, hotels or a family member's house. I'd strongly suggest avoiding the latter: a funeral can be emotionally exhausting and you want to be able to run away when necessary! The main things to arrange are the venue and potential catering – which can be as simple as asking people to bring dishes.

Inviting people to the funeral – and telling them about the death

Once the date is confirmed, you'll be able to invite guests. This may also be the first time you're telling some people about the death. To make this process somewhat easier, I suggest waiting to tell people about the death until you have a confirmed funeral date – it means you don't have to make contact twice with every person.

Next, decide who you want to tell personally about the death, and who can find out the news from someone else. Once you've made a list of people whom you're not telling personally, give that list to trusted friends. They can phone these people for you, and give them the news. Remember, nobody is going to begrudge you for not hearing this news firsthand.

If speaking on the phone feels too emotional, tell some people the news via text message. You can also mention that you'd prefer if they reply via text instead of calling you. People are usually eager to do whatever's easiest for you, but sometimes you'll have to tell them what that is.

When you share the news of a death with people, you'll probably hear the common phrase, "Please let me know if there's anything I can do..." It's a lovely gesture, but also such a vague statement. You can have a list of responses ready for that question: "Actually, I do need some help with telling others about the funeral/walking the dog/picking a child up from school/running errands..."

A death somehow gives you a free pass to ask for favours (more so than normal). People want to help, but don't know how to. If there's ever a time to cash in that help, then it's now.

Writing the eulogy

Putting your grief into words, especially so soon after a death, can be extremely difficult. Although there's no expectation for you to write and read a eulogy at a funeral, you might feel a certain amount of internal pressure, as their child, to be the one to do it. Remember that you can always write something and ask a friend to say it on the day; just make sure you have a copy written or printed out in case.

Typically, a eulogy is three to five minutes long. Depending on your speaking speed, that's approximately 1,000 words. It can feel like a massive task to distill someone's life like this. Think about it like a public goodbye letter: you're mentioning their best qualities and unforgettable characteristics along with their achievements and pivotal moments from their life. Don't be afraid to ask their friends and other family members to tell you their stories or memories too.

If you're not sure where to start, I'd suggest thinking about these questions:

- What was their childhood and upbringing like? Do you have any little anecdotes to share?
- What was your relationship with them like?
- What were their best qualities?
- Think about the various groups of funeral guests who knew them at different stages or in different facets of their life. What wouldn't they know about your parent?

Once you've got the framework, try reading it out loud. You'll get an idea of what sounds best. If you practice like this a few times you'll get used to the words, the speed, the rhythm, and when to pause for breath. It'll also lessen the chance of you getting unexpectedly emotional when reading it at the funeral.

Your experience of the funeral

The funeral is the culmination of the first weeks of grief. Your attention has been fixed on this event, on this date, for a while now, and there's every chance that it's become emotionally charged. In order to minimise the triggers brought on by the day, there are few things worth bearing in mind.

Call the funeral home a few days before to check there's nothing else you need to arrange or confirm, and to put your mind at ease.

Give yourself plenty of time to get to the funeral space. The last thing you want is to be rushing and worrying about being late. You can always wait in your car or walk around a bit until it's time to go inside.

When will you enter the space? Do you want to greet people at the doors or walk in at the last moment before the funeral starts?

Where will you sit during the service? A funeral director will usually reserve you a seat in the front row, but consider how close to the coffin you're comfortable being, and whether you'll have to cross in front of it to give the eulogy.

Are you comfortable with seeing the coffin being

carried in or out? You can ask for the coffin to be put in place before you arrive at the funeral, and to stay in place until after you've left.

Make sure that the people in your core support network know beforehand what you want or don't want to happen. Are there particular relatives or casual acquaintances who may trigger unwelcome emotions or memories? Do you want to avoid all conversation with guests until after the service? Explain your worries to your support network so they can form a protective barrier between you and unwanted situations.

Bring tissues and a bottle of water, put your phone on silent, and wear comfortable shoes. I find great comfort in holding my parents' possessions so I wore my mum's jewellery and my dad's comfy cardigan at the funeral. Even the smallest things can bring you comfort, and this is the day you need it.

The burial or cremation

A burial or cremation will happen after the service and is often at a separate site, which means funeral guests need to walk or drive there. Remember you don't have to include all guests at this part – you can ask many of them to head straight to the wake, and have a small group of your closest people at the graveside or in the crematorium. As with the funeral, you can ask the funeral director to lead you away from the grave before the coffin is lowered, or in the case of a cremation, to leave the coffin where it is until the congregation has left the space.

As this is the "final moment" where you're physically close to your parent, it can be a really emotional or even a traumatic part of the day. Hold tightly to a friend's hand and breathe deeply.

The wake

Once the funeral is over, you're allowed to feel a sense of relief. You might enjoy being able to talk at length about the person you've lost with those who knew them best – but if you're out of energy then nobody will mind if you sneak away. Remember, the funeral and the wake provide a shared space for people to come together and remember the deceased. You're not responsible for facilitating these conversations.

What to do after the funeral

Before you step into the murky world of emotional grief, there's more admin to be done. A person is involved with dozens of organisations during their lifetime, and all of them should be officially informed about the death. If not, you may continue to receive post with your parent's name on the address, or be forced to answer phone calls where a voice demands to speak to a person who's no longer alive. All this can be really triggering, particularly when it's unexpected. The easiest way to handle it is to make a big list, start making phone calls, and tick each organisation off as you go.

These are the elements of a person's life which you may need to cancel outright:

- Bank accounts – try to find account numbers, passwords to online banking and amounts in each account.
- Credit cards
- Council tax
- Car tax
- Car insurance
- Driving licence
- Phone and internet
- Passport
- Subscriptions (e.g. art galleries and museums.)

These are the things to switch into someone else's name (even if only for a transitory period):

- Utilities – water, gas and electricity bills. It's useful to know which bank accounts these are debited to, and their login info.

- House insurance
- Council tax
- Phone and internet services
- House mortgage (try and find the house deeds too.)

There are a few services which make it easier to inform multiple organisations at once. In the UK you can use the following:

- **Tell Us Once**: this reports a death to various departments of central and local government. This includes taxes, public pension, passport, driving licence, council tax, and removal from the electoral register.
- **Deceased Preference Service**: this stops unsolicited mail arriving, and helps protect the identity of the deceased.
- **The Bereavement Register**: this does the same as the above.

Closing their bank accounts

The most important thing to sort out is their bank accounts, as this is probably where you'll need to access funds to pay for the funeral. Be aware that when you report a death to the bank, they'll freeze the bank account. That means all direct debits will be stopped until the will is "proved", which could take a while.

You'll need to be able to cover necessary bills like utilities and council tax until then.

When closing accounts, banks will usually only take instruction from the executor of a will. If you're the executor then your name will be written on the front of the will, and this makes you responsible for dealing with all the official death admin: collecting assets, paying off debts and distributing the estate (which is all fancy talk for sorting out their stuff). If you're not the executor, then you'll need written permission from whoever it is – usually a lawyer, solicitor, next of kin or close friend.

Although it's possible to cancel accounts over the phone, I'd recommend going to the bank in person, as it feels a bit less overwhelming.

The documents you might need include:
- Original death certificate
- A copy of their will
- The funeral invoice on letter-headed paper (to pay the deposit)
- Your ID (passport or driving licence is best)
- Their national insurance number
- Their bank cards
- Any other relevant documents, e.g. house insurance, stocks, shares

Probate

Probate is the process of administering a dead person's estate: organising their money, assets and possessions, and distributing them as inheritance after you've paid off any taxes and debts. If you're the executor of the will, then it's your responsibility to take charge of this. It can feel like a scary thing to embark upon, probably because it's the most legal part of death admin.

In the UK, it's possible to complete probate yourself by filling out various forms (check the government's website for the correct forms) or you can hire a solicitor to do it.

If you decide on a probate solicitor as I did, my tips are as follows:

- Do your research. I spoke to a dozen different solicitors on the phone and made lots of notes about their individual offers.
- Different solicitors have different ways of pricing – some charge a set rate per hour, others charge one total sum.
- Get itemised quotes from each solicitor.
- Ask your network for anyone who might have some advice or experience.
- Meet with potential solicitors before deciding.

Once you've chosen your probate solicitor, they'll

need the following information:

- ○ Assets (house, car, bank accounts, jewellery, silver, furniture, and personal effects like computers and TVs.)
- ○ Debts (utility bills, council tax, internet, credit cards, and funeral expenses.)
- ○ Death certificate
- ○ Birth certificate
- ○ Marriage certificate
- ○ National insurance number or equivalent
- ○ Document proving state pension and benefits
- ○ Insurance policies
- ○ Deeds for any owned property
- ○ The original will (which you won't get back because they keep it) and multiple copies
- ○ House valuation (you may need a house surveyor to value the property.)

Tips for probate

Make digital and physical copies of all the above, and keep all the relevant paperwork in order.

I didn't feel comfortable sending my dad's will to the solicitors via recorded delivery, so I took it to the offices myself.

PART TWO

–

RESPONSES TO GRIEF

5

Emotional and Physical Reactions

After the funeral, you're in no man's land. As difficult as it may have felt to organise, the funeral acts as a necessary ritual to remember someone, and it's the one event you know will happen. It's also, probably, been the sole event you've focused your time and energy on since they died. You may not have thought beyond it. You might have half-imagined that they could still be alive and it's all been a bad dream. But once the funeral's over, your mind begins to catch up to the idea of what's happened. This is perhaps when true realisation begins to set in: the person you loved has actually gone.

After Mum's funeral, I went back to university in a

blurry, robotic state. Lectures, evenings in the pub, playing video games, and smoking a lot of weed with my then-boyfriend: everything felt very surreal, as if I was play-acting. At the time I didn't recognise the value of having the structure of academic life to follow, and I muddled through without connecting much to anyone or anything. I simply put my head down and tried to ignore the emotions snapping at my heels.

After Dad's funeral, I felt much more like a child than I had eight years earlier. Despite being responsible for sorting out all of the death admin, it was as if I'd regressed; I badly needed someone else to take the reins of my life and tell me what to do and where to go. My then-boyfriend was based in Scotland and needed to find a new place to live up there, and before Dad's terminal diagnosis I'd said I would move there too. So after the funeral, we went up to Scotland and spent a few weeks looking at apartments while hanging out with his friends. In hindsight, it was a mistake. I was terrified about the security of my empty house in London, I couldn't cope with being in unfamiliar surroundings, and I was so mentally and physically exhausted that I just wanted to press pause on everything. The world was moving much too quickly and I felt completely unanchored.

I'd made an unconscious decision to put aside all thinking about Dad as soon as the funeral was over –

then I suddenly broke down at a Christmas art fair in rural Scotland a month later, the emotions tumbling out of me. I couldn't stop crying. It was terrifying.

Grief is not linear - it's like a wave of conflicting emotions

Grief is scary, all-encompassing, overwhelming and a whole host of other buzzwords which never quite fit, and *who cares* about the correct definition, because you can't believe what's happening to you.

Perhaps the biggest thing you should know about grief is that it's non-linear. Although the Kübler-Ross "five stages of grief" are all applicable (both to a dying person and to those mourning their death), these emotions don't happen in a specific order and they don't happen just once. Along with denial, anger, bargaining, depression, and acceptance, you'll also encounter a multitude of other feelings – everything from apathy, avoidance, and guilt to fury, lethargy, and forgetfulness. And importantly, every single experience of grief is different. I thought I'd know how to handle my dad's death because I'd done "this whole grief thing" once before with Mum, but their two deaths provoked entirely different initial grief responses from me.

After Mum's death, I felt numb and confused, empty and sad. It was more passive than anything else. I consented to it without protest and just let it wash over me.

After Dad's death, I felt raw and ripped open, volatile and furious. It was entirely active and outward, with a hundred different emotions clamouring for attention inside me.

The common factor with both grieving processes? I wanted to be alone. My ability to mourn felt easiest and most natural if I was by myself, free to cry, scream, and make guttural animal noises in my throat which both terrified me and felt fundamentally appropriate. The way I cried was the same for both deaths, too. Even if the provoking emotions were contrasting, I still recognised the same tension in my chest, the same urge to expel something. I honestly think it's the same feeling as needing to vomit: a base human reaction which your body has more control over than your mind.

But perhaps because it's physical more than mental, the sheer intensity of my grief has frightened me on multiple occasions. There have been solid blocks of days when I haven't left my house, waking up in tears and staying huddled under the duvet for hours, crawling on my hands and knees to the bathroom, or standing in the kitchen to make some poor attempt at food and suddenly falling to the floor again. I've felt like an absurd overdramatic actress, and seen myself out-of-body and wanted to laugh – but I've also felt this intensity was necessary.

From my experience, grief is like a wave. It rises up and then falls, only to rise again a few hours, days or weeks later. Riding that wave, accepting there'll be consecutive days which fully overwhelm me before the intensity recedes again, has been the best way through.

Because despite your grief, the normal world can and does continue. For short snatches of time, you almost forget what's happened. You switch to autopilot: brush your teeth, choose your clothes, catch the train, eat your meals, meet your friends. You laugh and joke; you schedule appointments; you slip back into normality. But it's always there, this new version of reality which weighs your body down, and every reminder stings as if you're learning about it for the first time.

Your world has changed. Now comes the hard task of re-adjusting yourself and your life to what this new world looks like.

Feeling numb

When someone dies, you might feel absolutely nothing. The shock of death is very real – too real to actually take in – and the reigning emotion may be emptiness. Apathy. Your mind and body don't have the resilience or capacity to always dwell on death. Much like when you break a bone and don't feel the pain for a while, there will be whole hours or even days when you're operating on a relatively normal level. That's usually when the phone rings and you hear a grieving voice say, "Oh darling, how *are* you..."

Although it can be something of a relief to feel numbness in grief, the downside is that people expect you to be feeling *all* of the things. And if you don't, it can feel rather worrying.

Avoidance

It's common to go into survival mode and block out the true enormity of what's happened. This can be a conscious decision or entirely unconscious – and the latter means you may well not realise it's even happening. You might look for distraction, immediately heading back to work and telling everyone you're doing fine. You might also be a bit more dramatic about it. My way of coping with Mum's death was to go travelling by myself, in the naive hope that grief would somehow pass me by while I wasn't focusing on it. Eventually, grief found me regardless. It took seven years for me to truly begin confronting the significance of Mum's death in my life, and it was all the more difficult because I'd left it so long. As a result, when I knew Dad was dying I resolved to not avoid my grief, however overwhelming it might be.

Exhaustion and lethargy

In the days following my dad's death, I woke up and couldn't leave my bed for hours. No matter how hard I tried, my brain wouldn't switch on. I begrudgingly accepted this state because there wasn't another option, but it was awful to feel so impotent. The horrible irony? Although I was always tired, actually trying to sleep at night was difficult, and eventually I feared bedtime, knowing I'd have to lie awake for hours before my mind eventually shut itself off.

Grief exhaustion is a very real thing. Even routine tasks feel like too much effort. I was barely able to get dressed, would spend a panicked hour growing steadily hungrier while knowing I couldn't find the tiniest spark of energy to make myself food, and the idea of showering was simply too much. It felt like nothingness, or a strange period of waiting – but for what, I didn't know. Strangely, this is when the death admin was actually helpful. I could focus the little energy I had on performing one task successfully – then I could feel I'd at least achieved one useful thing that day.

Grief fog

There are days which seem to disappear, and minutes which feel like hours. You might find yourself in the kitchen waiting for the kettle to boil and not remember how you got there, or even where you were before. You can't concentrate, you forget names and dates, and you feel bizarre asking your friends to repeat themselves because you don't remember what they've just said.

Initially, I called this my goldfish memory, but eventually I renamed it "the grief fog". It's a scary thing to feel you're losing grip on your memory. *Am I going crazy? Is this what life will be like from now on?* I chalk it up to the fact that my brain was so overwhelmed – first by anticipatory grief, and then by trying to make sense of my loss – that there was simply no space for remembering rudimentary information.

Vulnerability

Unfortunately, the grief fog also means you're

constantly re-reminded that they're gone. It feels like your mind is stuck in perpetual reboot mode, so a fresh wave of "Oh my god, they actually DIED?!" can happen multiple times a day, and each time feels like the first. How on earth was I ever going to cope with this? More importantly, how was I ever going to *understand* that I had to cope with this?

As the full enormity of having to live my life without my parents repeatedly made its impact, it chipped away at my capacity to cope. I felt raw and exposed, as if my skin was paper-thin. I could feel tears constantly pressing on the backs of my eyes like floodgates threatening to burst. I knew that the tiniest trigger could easily push me over the edge, and that made me feel so vulnerable. My anxiety skyrocketed during this time because I was acutely aware that anything – a stranger pushing past me, catching my fingernail on something, a sudden unexpected noise, even someone looking at me with annoyance – would cause me to start sobbing.

In public, I would desperately try to hold the emotion back. I couldn't bear the thought of strangers seeing me break down in the middle of the street. But when I was alone and I allowed myself to cry, it was a really scary experience. That unrestrained outpouring of emotion felt animalistic: a no-holds-barred, guttural, close-to-vomiting style of crying which took over my whole body. I often worried about the depth of my sadness. I felt that, if I truly let go the way my body seemed to want me to, I might never stop – like opening up a Pandora's Box of grief.

Fear, anxiety and 'fight or flight' mode

The acute vulnerability I felt while grieving made me very protective of my emotions. I was worried that crying might strike at any time, so I began to judge every situation based on how easily I could find a private space to cry if necessary. Taking long journeys on public transport made me anxious; I didn't want to go too far from home or the places I felt safe, and soon I stopped doing anything which held the possibility of danger. Even going to see my therapist was too stressful and exhausting. Her sessions were over an hour from my house, using three different types of transport, and I couldn't deal with the unknowns of that commute without having a panic attack. For someone who travels independently around the world for a living, this anxiety was a stark contrast to my sense of what felt normal.

I think much of my anxiety stemmed from the supreme lack of confidence I felt after Mum's death. She was my constant cheerleader no matter what I did, and to suddenly lose someone's unwavering faith in your abilities can inflict a lot of damage. When it was coupled with the realisation that terrible things really can happen in life, I lost trust in the world around me. Suddenly I was scared of *so much*. I developed a fear of falling down flights of stairs, began to hate turbulence when flying, and became acutely aware of totally mundane situations which could harm or kill me.

Of course, the world is still the same as it always was, but living through something seriously traumatic forces your perception of the world to change.

Hypervigilance and hyperarousal are common side effects of grief. Your body becomes acutely familiar with the signals for panic and throws you into high-intensity "fight or flight" mode with any possible prompt. "That dodgy-looking guy could punch you! That fast car could swerve and hit you! Better be prepared for drama because you *never know*!" These responses become second-nature very quickly, and they're pretty hard to pull away from. Two years after Dad's death, I still flinch at any movement out of the corner of my eye. I'm easily startled by unexpected noises or activity. I'm often tense and on edge for no real reason and I find it difficult to relax.

Loneliness and isolation

Perhaps my biggest realisation about grief was how utterly lonely it can be – something I never truly realised until I was immersed in it. The combination of these big emotions and thoughts happening all at once can highlight just how different your situation is to everyone else around you.

I'd often stare at people walking past me and feel dumbstruck. Were they seriously not aware of all the ways they could die, or be hurt, or be forced to watch the pain of those they loved with no way of stopping it? How were they just carrying on as normal? How did the very possibility of grief not flatten them where they stood? It was as if I lived in a fundamentally different world which nobody else could understand.

The swift switching in my emotions was unnerving and added to my loneliness. I could be fine one minute, furious the next, and devastatingly sad a moment later. I didn't trust my ability to stay in one mood for more than a few minutes at a time, and it led to cancelling plans with anyone other than my closest friends. Even seeing them was difficult, because however well-meaning my friends were, there came a point when I couldn't keep explaining the same sadnesses and worries and fears.

It's painfully ironic that the only people I wanted to

comfort me about my parents' deaths were my parents.

I desperately wanted my mum to tell me everything would be OK. Even after Dad's death, when she'd been gone for almost a decade, I still half-expected her to magically appear and fix everything.

Being around people allows us to pretend we're doing OK – and for a while we might even believe the front we're presenting to the world. For some, that really helps to contain the emotion. But it can be exhausting and isolating to keep up this pretence, and being alone is often where we're able to allow grief to do its thing.

Once self-imposed isolation begins to happen, you're left alone with your thoughts – and I often turned to an almost martyr-like thought pattern. "Nobody knows me like my parents did," I'd think, bitterly. "I'll never have that easy familiar connection with anyone again." That was a huge isolator for me. I ached for the ability to relax in someone's company, knowing I could say or do anything in unwavering faith that they'd still love me. It was devastating to know I could never do that with my parents again. I felt excluded from the ease of family which the rest of the world still seemed to have, and which I no longer did.

Irritation, anger, and fury

The anger I felt after Dad's death was like a heavy vessel of hot liquid in my chest. It usually sat simmering in the background, but occasionally it would jolt and spill over, and at that point my emotions went from zero to a hundred in mere seconds. Suddenly I wanted furious revenge on the stranger who'd been stupid enough to walk into me on the street, or the well-meaning casual acquaintance who'd dared to say something about grief which I didn't agree with. I was scared of the level of anger I held inside me. I didn't expect it, and I didn't know what it might lead to.

We think we're supposed to bottle up our volatile emotions, but you are absolutely allowed to be angry in grief. You've experienced a death which you were powerless to stop, and that impotence can easily fill you with rage. So feel your fury. Allow it to exist. Let those burning, heated sparks fly – but perhaps try to scream into pillows instead of screaming at strangers.

Guilt

Guilt is a common and complex emotion to feel after someone dies. You might feel guilty for not doing or saying enough when they were alive; guilty about how much grief is affecting you or how long it's lasting. In the case of my dad's death, I felt guilty because I was relieved it was finally over. It took a while for me to actually express that out loud - I thought people would interpret it to mean that I'd wanted him to die. But the exhausted terror-state I lived in for eight months, watching such a proud man steadily lose his autonomy, was horrible, and I can't imagine how much worse it felt for him. It's OK to want the dying process to be over. It doesn't mean you love them any less.

A lot of people have also told me they feel guilty or ashamed for "still" feeling overwhelmed with grief when it's been six months, or two years, or a decade since their person died. That's totally fine! Never let anyone influence your grief. It takes as long as it takes, and it will come back and forth in waves, probably for the rest of your life. The timespan of your grief is nothing to feel guilty about.

To cope with your grief emotions, let go of the "shoulds"

It's important to remember that whatever emotions you feel are completely valid. They are all appropriate (even if they don't feel like it). They're all allowed to exist. If you need to cry, let it happen. If you feel strangely calm, relish that state. If you're exhausted and need to spend a lot of time in bed, that's fine too. Give yourself permission to feel whatever you're feeling.

If possible, try and let go of the shoulds. "I should be doing better. I should be able to meet that person for dinner. I shouldn't spend all day in bed. I shouldn't be crying this much..." An anxious person's life is often disrupted by second-guessing their actions. I question my decisions regularly – but I've recently begun to realise that everything's much easier if I just let that shit go. Don't look ahead to next month, or next week, or even to the end of today. Just think about what the next few minutes hold for you.

Aim to be kind and compassionate to yourself. Think of yourself as a car crash victim whose injuries aren't visible to other people. You still need rest and rehabilitation, but it's up to you to decide what that looks like. I spent so much on takeaways from Deliveroo in the first few months after Dad's death. My ability to buy groceries, much less cook them, went totally out of the window, so I gave myself a free pass to indulge in all the comfort food I wanted.

Track your moods to see the patterns and trajectory of your grief

My most-used phrase when describing my grief was probably "the feelings and emotions just come out of nowhere." It's a bizarre sensation: barely there for weeks on end and then suddenly, one day, BAM! You can barely move for the enormity of it, you can barely breathe for crying, and you can't imagine how you ever felt OK before this. It's the sudden surprise that makes it feel so sharp – but over time you might start to see a pattern to how your grief moves, and this can be really helpful for minimising how overwhelmed you feel in response.

My grief ebbs and flows like water at the shoreline. I'll have a few days of feeling all right, a few days when the skies seem to darken and my mood declines, a few days of unstoppable crying and sadness, and then my mood starts to lift again.

I've begun to recognise the symptoms which mean I'm in a decline: I get despondent, irritable and withdrawn, I can't focus on my work, and the biggest tell is when I feel like showering is too much effort. But more importantly, I also know these symptoms have always eventually faded, which means that when I feel them rising and threatening to overwhelm me, I can hold on to the awareness that I've made it through before, and will do again.

In my mind, the path of grief looks like a series of peaks (good days) and valleys (bad days). At first the valleys last way longer and the peaks are tiny moments, but gradually you'll have higher, longer peaks and shallower, shorter valleys. If you start noticing a pattern, you can try to use your better days for doing death admin so your worse days don't feel so pressured.

Pay attention to your body - physical grief is a real thing

My mind is often at odds with my physical self. There's an overwhelming sadness which tells me repeatedly that I'm much too devastated to even consider stepping outside – even though I feel my muscles twitch with the need for activity and movement. Then again, sometimes my body knows exactly what's happening before my mind does; lethargy indicates the start of a depressive phase, and getting an infection reminds me I'm pushing myself too hard and need to step back.

In the first year after Dad died, I got multiple cold sores, developed an aching hip, and my jaw locked itself shut for almost a week because my muscles were so tense. My body was crying out for attention, trying to tell me that I wasn't looking after myself as well as I could. That was pretty overwhelming in itself! But it was also a good wake-up call that I had to re-adjust my self-care practices.

I began to listen to my body, registering how it felt when emotion was building inside my chest. I became familiar with the way the tears rose in my throat and prickled behind my eyes. I gave my body the chance to tell me what was wrong – and then I made adjustments to the way I lived. To combat my difficulties with sleeping, I stopped drinking coffee and tried my best to establish a screen-free nighttime routine, choosing to read a book in bed instead. Whenever my heart began to race with no provocation, I actively stopped what I was doing, took a few deep breaths and tried to focus on calm, serene thoughts. Remember that your cells have gone through trauma, and it takes a visible toll – my hair even started going grey in the months after Mum's death. It's not just your mind which needs to grieve; your body has to grieve too.

Grief can affect your sex life

Many people turn to sex as an antidote for grief. It makes sense: if you've lost a central source of intimacy in your life, like the love of a parent, you may instinctively seek out intimacy in other forms. But it's just as common to lose interest in sex altogether, or for your libido to behave erratically. When my dad died, I was in a long-distance relationship. Sometimes I'd be desperate to have sex with my partner when we saw each other, while other weeks I was apprehensive about seeing him because I knew it was almost expected that I "should" want to be intimate, and I knew I couldn't be.

It's distressing to have no control over your sex drive. I didn't understand the arbitrary rules my body was making. I usually wanted affection in the form of words, attention and kindness, but often I couldn't even bear to be hugged or touched in bed. Intimacy in any form was too real and too raw. The added pressure of not wanting to hurt my partner's feelings or make him think any of this was his fault quickly became another stress factor.

Just as the erratic nature of your grief eventually settles, so will your libido. I eventually realised that I was equating sex with pleasure and vulnerability – two emotions I was desperately trying not to allow myself, in case I felt more pain as a result.

Exercise and movement does help

The clichés are annoyingly true: when you're feeling awful, getting outside and moving your body can do you the world of good. I've attempted the running programme Couch to 5k multiple times, but even if I hate the idea of getting into exercise clothes and going to the park, I do feel happier once I'm moving my feet.

That said, when I'm deep in the midst of grieving, proactive sport is often too much to face. That's when the smallest amount of effort, practiced with a ton of self-care and compassion, is just as good. During a few big crying sessions, I've managed to put a jacket on and walk around the block – and doing this in the rain was strangely satisfying because it hid the tears which rolled down my face.

The positive effects of passive sensory overload

Sometimes movement can be too much and you might need a distraction to pull you away from feeling miserable. After my dad died, I binge-watched every Netflix show I could think of – everything from prison dramas like *Orange Is The New Black* and apocalyptic zombie outbreaks like *The Walking Dead* to gory hospital soap operas like *Grey's Anatomy* and violent drug-fuelled dramas like *Breaking Bad*. I watched some comedy too (endless reruns of *Friends* are like balm for me!), but bizarrely enough, it was watching constant dramatic deaths on TV which felt the most therapeutic. That style of show numbs me to the concept of death, reminding me that thousands of people die every day (whether fictional or in real life), and it allows me a confined timeframe in which to cry. For ten minutes, scriptwriters and cast actively want their viewer to be upset, whether at the scene or their own issues, but then the scene changes and suddenly my sadness lifts again.

Find comfort in daily structure or routine

Routine was never something I craved, and when my mum died I actively denied myself any kind of structure. I felt that if I kept moving, kept travelling, I'd somehow shrug off the grieving period. Although that didn't work in the long run, for a long time I felt protected from grief because I was always challenged by the relatively low-key issues of life on the road.

However, after the constant "what-if" moments throughout my dad's decline, I've now discovered I feel most calm when my life has an obvious structure. I meditate each morning. I make toast and coffee in my kitchen. I reply to emails, settle down to writing, eat lunch, go for a run, see friends in the evenings. It's normal and familiar, and ten years ago was something I never thought I'd want!

If you've been through trauma which involved many moments of unexpected difficulty, routine helps you build a sense of security back into your life – and it's also a good way to regain some control. Knowing where my toothbrush is, knowing what food is in my fridge and what meals I'm cooking that week: having a familiar set of movements throughout the day allows my mind to perform these things almost unconsciously, and I feel more relaxed as a result.

Find your safe, private spaces to grieve in

Feeling safe is so important during the first waves of grief. For me, a "safe space" means somewhere I can cry without judgement or embarrassment. Usually, it's when I'm in my family house; most often, it's when I'm alone. There are two parks within walking distance from my house, and I know the particular benches I like to sit on because being there makes me feel calm. I have keys to my best friend's house, along with an open invitation to drop in anytime. I know how to recognise that rising feeling of panic when I'm on a bus or a train, and I know that if I check Google Maps to find somewhere quiet, green, and spacious close by, it will let me feel a little better.

6

Other People's Reactions to Your Grief

Coping with your own grief is awful, but at least it only involves you. When you bring other people into the mix, though, it can get complicated.

Even with the best intentions in the world, many people just don't behave the way you want or need them to when confronted with the topic of grief. It makes my heart sink when I'm introduced to a stranger and I know I'll have to have "the conversation" about my parents. My choices are limited: it's either tell them the truth and incite a possible awkward moment, or decide to lie about the deaths I've gone through – which can throw a whole new set of guilty emotions into the mix!

Our attitude to death and grief is, in the western world at least, completely backward. We're hidden from the painful, complicated parts of a fundamental part of everyone's life experience until it's unavoidable. The only time you talk about grief is when you're actively going through it. It means we have absolutely no idea how to behave towards the grieving. I've written more about how we talk about death in Chapter 13, but these are the most common situations I've had to navigate.

First, there are the people who are blindsided by the fact that your parent has died and immediately want to run away from the conversation. You see it in their body language and their awkward lack of eye contact; they don't know what to say, and bizarrely it's you, the griever, who feels obligated to make them feel better about the much-too-serious topic they've stumbled into. This can have some serious side effects and even lead to the loss of a relationship. A girl at university ignored me for a month after my mum died, even though we lived in the same house. Eventually, she told me she'd felt too awkward and sad to say anything at all – but by then the damage had been done, and our friendship fizzled out soon after.

Then there are the people who ask questions about how it happened, what the cause of death was, and how you're managing to cope. They don't mean to sound voyeuristic; it's a normal human reaction to be curious about a part of life they haven't experienced yet. Some people also seem to feel awkwardly obligated to talk about it once they know what's happened! But if these people aren't able to pick up your subtle hints – either that you don't want to talk about it, or that they've asked one question too many – it can get really upsetting. Having a short auto-explanation about my parents has served me well (I discuss this further in Chapter 14). The words are so familiar now that saying them out loud doesn't impact me the way it used to.

There are also the lovely yet misguided people who try to make things better, but who only succeed in making you feel worse. Again, it's human nature to try and fix the problem – but what these well-meaning folks haven't realised is that death is the one thing in the world which is impossible to fix. The number of times I heard, "It'll all be OK," which made me want to scream, "How on earth can you possibly think that?!" It took me a long time to realise why this phrase infuriated me so much, but I think I've got it now: hearing "it'll be OK" suggests the person is effectively bypassing all the pain of my current grief to focus on a future which feels extremely far away. I don't need comfort about what my future self might feel – my current self needs help with this current pain right now!

But the reactions which impact me the most are from people who have absolutely no idea what's happened. One afternoon I stood at the automated checkout at the supermarket, fighting back the tears which rose in my throat. The machine wasn't working. A cashier told me to scan the food again. It didn't work. As the cashier's voice grew steadily more irritable, I just wanted to scream, "My dad is dying at home! I don't know what I'm doing! Please stop being mean to me!" Of course, there's no way she could have known what was happening in my life – but that thought didn't help at the time.

Grief is completely invisible to the world at large and can often feel extremely frustrating. The Victorians used to wear a black armband or dress completely in black so anyone they passed knew they were in mourning. I felt as if I wanted to wear a sandwich board proclaiming that my dad was dead – perhaps with a counter of how many days I'd been grieving for. I needed people to understand the sheer magnitude of the loss I was navigating.

We all develop our own methods for explaining our grief to others, but bear in mind that it's your choice to direct those conversations in ways that work for you. In fact, it's often better to be the one in control. I've become more bolshy when it comes to dictating conversations around grief. If I'm in the mood to talk about my parents, fine. And if not? I say, "Actually I'd much prefer talking about something happier, if that's OK." You can see the relief in people's eyes when they realise you've taken the reins!

You're allowed to tell people they're not being helpful or when they're actively making you feel bad. You're allowed to be angry when people don't understand the boundaries of your grief. You don't have to be considerate towards other people's awkward feelings about your grief. Most importantly, you do not owe anyone your sadness. This grief is yours to process in whatever way you can. Don't feel compelled or pressured to act how anyone else expects you to.

7

Home and Possessions

We only ever lived in one house as a family. During the years after Mum died, my dad methodically cleared her piles of tatty *Hello* magazines from the bathroom, the old newspapers stuffed underneath the bed, and the dozens of bulging plastic bags from the backs of dusty cupboards, re-organising our family house in a way which suited his newly-solo and much neater life. But Dad didn't get rid of everything Mum had owned and loved. He knew that I'd want to make the decisions about some of her possessions, so I was responsible for sorting through the majority of Mum's personal stuff and deciding what to keep.

I quickly amassed a collection of Mum's chunky knitted cardigans and baggy jumpers, hand-painted earrings and antique necklaces, and plenty of the worn leather handbags she'd picked up in Florence decades earlier. Since her death, I've absorbed Mum's possessions into my own wardrobe so successfully that it often takes me a minute to remember they were hers when someone asks. But it never fails to bring me a little thrill of happiness to say, "These earrings? Yeah, they were my mum's – aren't they gorgeous?"

I spent intermittent months living in the family house during the decade between my parents' deaths, but when Dad's death was imminent I moved back home properly. Although my childhood bedroom was empty, the narrow single bed – and the room's proximity to my dying dad just next door – wasn't at all tempting. So the living room downstairs became my temporary bedroom for almost a year. I folded out the sofa into a rudimentary bed, balanced my makeup and moisturisers on top of Mum's closed record player, laid out my own bits and pieces amongst the candlesticks and postcards on the mantelpiece, and cleared cupboards of board games and school art projects to make way for piles of my folded-up clothes. It wasn't a positive experience to live like this, but it did highlight how easy the clearing out of a familiar space can be when it's suddenly necessary.

For years I'd felt moving too much of my mum's stuff would be somehow disrespectful – but when push came to shove and there wasn't another choice, I found it strangely liberating. Late into the evening, I would sit cross-legged on the floor, sifting through piles of my old school work which Mum had dutifully kept, yet which I had no connection to. It felt cathartic to chuck tons of it into the bin, and in no time the living room became the first place in the house which didn't actively remind me of my parents – the reclamation of a space I didn't think I needed to reclaim.

Although Dad died at a hospice instead of at home, it still took several months before I dared to go into his bedroom upstairs. Once the hospital-style bed had been removed the room was much too empty, and I felt strange standing in there – almost as if the air had expanded, rushing into every possible gap. It was much too painful to be in that space without him in it. But eventually my connection to the space changed, and now that bedroom is mine. I re-organised the furniture, got rid of a chest of drawers, successfully constructed a bed frame entirely on my own, and bought myself the biggest mattress known to man to put on it. After lots of internal debating, I made an active choice to continue living alone in the house I grew up in. It was difficult at first – there are still dozens of reminders of my parents in every room and I'm often floored by the sudden influx of associated memories – but I've slowly grown used to calling this place "my house". Even using that new vocabulary, instead of saying "my dad's house", was a big step.

What do you do with the physical elements of someone's life when they no longer exist?

Sorting through a person's belongings is emotionally taxing and often triggering. You never know what emotions will be brought to the surface, so it's understandable to be scared of embarking on this process. But ironically there's also a part of grief that pushes you to find these memories and connections because you feel just a little closer to the person you miss so much.

The physical remnants of someone's life take on a strange quality after they die. What used to be nothing more than a hairbrush is suddenly an intimate object with an invaluable connection to the one you've lost. What was once a bricks-and-mortar building is now filled with shadowy memories which can suddenly become solid and catch you off guard. Yet not all objects are worth the same. While some quickly become talismans, others lose their importance once their original owner no longer holds onto them. Deciding whether something is emotionally valuable or not can take a while – and unfortunately, the mechanisms of grief mean you're thrown into making those decisions when you're already feeling emotional.

In the early stages of grief, you might find yourself spending entire evenings sitting on the carpet surrounded by their stuff. You're fuelled by a sudden sense of purpose, and you've gathered dusty photo albums, old notebooks, and dozens of their home-recorded VHS tapes. You've begun sorting through them. It feels beneficial, like you're achieving something significant. Like you're breaking the fear of What To Do With Their Stuff. And then, all at once, you're exhausted. Realising the enormity of what you're doing can be a lot to handle, and I've often had to abandon sorting sessions halfway through, leaving little piles of possessions around the house.

This overwhelm is compounded by the realisation that you've now become the sole keeper of all these memories. You don't want to disrupt the physical spaces they inhabited in case it makes you forget something important about them. Or anything at all – because once you forget, it's gone forever, and that seems too desperately sad.

A row of little green glass bottles sit above a closed-off doorway in my kitchen, and I still can't bear to move them because I know my mum decided they belonged there. She was the last person to touch them, and although it's been over a decade, I still can't be responsible for changing that.

My best advice is to take it slow. There's a self-inflicted pressure to sort through everything at once, but give yourself time to adjust. What their possessions mean to you today might be different next month, or next year; things which seem priceless now may end up being less precious later on. Letting go of their possessions is a form of saying goodbye, and as long as there's no immediate time pressure like selling their house, this process can take as long as you need it to.

What possessions do you want to keep?

We all have different connections to specific items, and sometimes the most unexpected objects have memories attached to them. As a starting point, I'd recommend the following:

Keep their handwriting

You might find it comforting to keep anything that features their handwriting. For me, finding any scrap of paper with my mum's distinctively messy scrawl or my dad's carefully-formed letters is like gold dust. There are shopping lists and Post-It Notes, a dozen of Mum's little gift tags for Christmas presents which say, "We love you inordinately!!", notebooks filled with twenty years of Dad's book reviews in his tiny neat script – and I kept them all. I even have a sentence my mum always used to say to me tattooed around my wrist, which I copied straight from a birthday card. Even after ten years, the shape of Mum's letters brings her right into my mind whenever I look at them.

Print off their emails

During my years of long-term travel, my dad and I would email all the time. After his death, I went through his email inbox (which felt only somewhat invasive) and forwarded various emails to my own inbox. Why? Because email addresses, social media accounts and phone numbers will eventually be cut off by the service providers – and it's usually earlier than you think. I listened repeatedly to the last voicemail my mum left me until it vanished after a few weeks because I'd never thought to try and save it. I'd recommend backing up their photos, phones, email accounts and anything else tech-related onto external hard drives. It's devastating when something like that is lost.

Wear their clothes and jewellery

I feel much closer to my parents when I remember I'm

wearing my mum's earrings or my dad's jumper. It's such a comforting way to keep their memory alive. However, if you don't feel quite right wearing their clothes (or they simply don't fit or suit you!) then you can turn their favourite shirts into cushion covers or their cardigans into bedspreads. There are plenty of similar ideas online.

When the entire house becomes a memory

My family house means more to me now than it ever has. It's been the fundamental constant throughout my life: first a place of ultimate familiarity and comfort, then a place to grieve with my dad about the loss of my mum, then a place to calmly remember her, then a place to watch my dad's declining health, then a place to grieve for him alone and rebuild my life again.

I'm surrounded by photos and objects and furniture and memories at every turn, which all act as beautiful and heartbreaking reminders of those I've lost. There are so many tiny details which mean everything to me but absolutely nothing to anybody else. The orange and blue shadows falling onto the bathroom floor every afternoon when the sun is shining through the stained-glass window. The chipped paint on the bannisters in the hall where we used to leave Post-It Notes for each other, explaining what we were up to that evening: her choir practices, my music lessons, his theatre rehearsals. The wild blackberries which have always grown in the garden, and which Dad would bake into a fruit crumble in the autumn, along with shop-bought apples and a secret ingredient of canned mango to make it smooth and creamy.

My family house feels like an anchor. When I reach a particular spot on the stairs, I can still see the half-memory of my dad sitting in his chair in the study. Sometimes at night there's a reflection in the kitchen window and it takes on the shape of my mum. If memories have a physical form, they exist most strongly in this house. It's like a holding space for my parents: the one place I know I can still "see" them if I want to. And yet I have a hundred questions about the house to which I can never know the answers. Where did they find the little painted cherub which hangs above the stairs? Why didn't Dad tell me how to unlock the second set of garden doors, or show me where the keys are hiding? How do I fix the strange leaking patches in the ceiling?

Many grieving people aren't in my position: they didn't live with their parent when they died, and they aren't planning on moving into the empty house. Maybe the place now feels too big for them to consider living there, or it's simply too upsetting. Problematically, another very common situation is being forced to sell the property in order to settle the person's estate. If you didn't live with them, or you have to sell the house quickly, then sorting through their possessions might have to be a rushed process. The tips below can help with minimising the emotional impact:

Clearing out their home can be therapeutic - but it might be overwhelming too

I've found that if I plan a clear-out in advance, I get emotional in anticipation – but the easiest and more successful clear-outs happen when I make a snap decision to do it on a Tuesday afternoon. That said, getting emotional isn't necessarily a bad thing. If you're trying not to think about their death then it's hard to imagine any positivity from sorting through their stuff, but when your mind switches into organisational mode, it actually seems to minimise the emotion a bit.

Choose a donation recipient that resonates with you

I donate the vast majority of my clear-outs to my local St Christopher's Hospice charity shop. Both of my parents spent their last days at that hospice, so it feels wonderful to have that link and to know the sale of their possessions is directly benefiting future residents.

Ask a charity to pick donations up

If it feels too stressful or overwhelming to take bags full of donations to your local charity shop, or if your donations include heavy or bulky furniture, you're in luck - many charities will come and pick up items from your house. You'll probably have to book in a collection slot and tell them ahead of time what you're planning to donate. Make sure you check any upholstered furniture for fire safety labels too, as they won't be accepted otherwise.

Hire a bereavement house clearance service

If you're really struggling to sift through possessions and decide what to keep, throw or donate, you can hire a house clearance service to do the job for you. They're often linked with an estate agent, so be prepared for probing questions about when you plan to sell the property, but if you aren't emotionally invested in most of the possessions this could be a good option.

Put stuff into storage

The last resort is to hire a storage space and chuck everything in there, so you can wait until you're less emotional to sort through it.

Ask someone to help you

When I've had trouble sorting through some rooms of the house, I've called in reinforcements: one friend to hand me half-forgotten objects from a cupboard, and another friend to take things from me once I've made a decision about whether or not to keep them. For those who attribute emotional weight to physical objects as I do, being speedy and making snap decisions is a helpful approach. Just remember that you're absolutely allowed to hesitate! The possessions which resonate with you now might feel different later. If you have the space to store them, there's nothing wrong with keeping hold of things and reassessing their meaning to you at a later date. I've had multiple clear-outs over the last decade, and it's meant I've been able to easily donate something which a few years earlier I felt a strong connection to.

8

Grief Triggers

In the first weeks and months after Mum's death, I saw her everywhere. Her curly red hair appeared ahead of me in crowds, her hand wrapped around the yellow pole of a tube train, her voice called my name in a supermarket. In later years, when the sightings had stopped, I often dreamed of her; confusing dreams which all followed the same narrative. It seemed I'd got things wrong and her death was all just a misunderstanding. Mum would appear in her usual way, so immediately familiar and absolutely *there* that I'd accept it as fact with a stunning sense of relief. And then I'd wake up and have to confront her loss yet again.

After Dad died, he joined those dreams. On those nights, I have to contend with a sudden re-adjusted world where my house has two more residents. I have to give up my bed to my parents, and explain to myself why I'd somehow thought they were dead all this time. I used to enjoy these dreams because it meant I got to see my mum – but now they're often more frustrating than anything else. If they involve anything more than mundanity, these dreams are one of my most unwelcome grief triggers. Whenever I wake after one, I feel unsettled and emotional, and it can take a while to get myself back to normal again.

At their heart, grief triggers are things that provoke memories about your loss. But they're more intense than normal memories: they're heavy, solid, hard to move away from, and they have the power to overwhelm you. It's a potent mixture of longing, love, sadness, and acute remembering. In my worst moments, those triggers precipitate a sudden desperation to see them, hug them, hear their voice, and to have just five minutes to tell them my news.

I've said that grief feels like a wave – but at these moments, it's more like a tsunami.

In my experience, grief triggers seem to fit into three categories: general death-related triggers, person-specific triggers, and completely unexpected triggers.

General death triggers are perhaps the easiest to contend with because they're predictable, and you can research ahead of time to know what might affect you. Common ones include books and films containing scenes of a dying parent, Mother's Day and Father's Day, and almost inevitably Christmas and your birthday. These are the obvious moments where you'll miss your parents most.

The person-specific triggers are harder to predict, but once you've faced them for the first time it can be easier. I know my birthday usually triggers me, and so does my Dad's birthday (also his death-day), yet I have barely any emotional connection to my mum's birthday or death-day. No idea why. There's also plenty of cultural triggers: their favourite song or movie, a particular place you always visited together, a delicious meal they used to make for you.

But it's the unexpected triggers which are usually the most upsetting. Because you never really know when they'll strike, the ensuing emotion feels more dramatic and more painful. These triggers can come from seemingly innocuous things – whenever I see vanilla creme crowns for sale, I remember it was the only thing my dad wanted to eat in his final days – or even worse, triggers can simply pop into your head for no reason at all. As mentioned in Chapter 5, you may find yourself always on high alert, waiting for something to set you off. The triggers themselves make you feel anxious, but so does the idea of being triggered! It's why I spent so much time at home the year after Dad died, because I didn't want to step outside and risk being triggered into unexpected grief. It's why living in another country for a year after Mum's death was so cathartic for me, because there were so few triggers of her in San Francisco.

General grief triggers

Anything to do with death or dying can be a grief trigger. So can anything which mimics the relationship you've lost. It means I've learned to avoid dozens of books and movies which include dying parents, or close mother-daughter relationships. I mute the TV when there's an advert for a funeral home or a warning PSA on the symptoms of a stroke. I watched the opening montage to *Up* once, and immediately vowed never to watch it again!

But you can't always avoid these general triggers. On one memorable Valentine's Day, two months after Mum died, my boyfriend and I rushed into the cinema a few minutes late and grabbed a couple of seats right at the front. From there I had an unobscured view of Benjamin Button's mum dying in childbirth. After less than ten minutes of the film, I was in floods of tears and had to leave. I remember the shock of realising that I'd have to be aware of triggers like this for potentially the rest of my life.

Annoyingly, it happens with just as many positive and happy situations as it does with sad ones. My blood will often burn at pregnancies, engagement announcements, and weddings – all things I know I'll never be able to share with my parents.

And then there are the annual occasions which I could spend all year feeling anxious about if I didn't work hard to stop myself. When Mum was alive, she used to celebrate every possible holiday. I'd come downstairs on Valentine's Day to see red-wrapped chocolate hearts scattered all over the table. At Easter, there were cuddly bunnies and yellow confetti everywhere. Handwritten cards arrived through the mail to congratulate me for piano exams and school plays. Mother's Day was the only occasion each year where Dad and I had to try and match her over-exuberance! But Christmas was my family's biggest celebration. Mum put sprigs of holly on all the picture frames, decorated the tree with ornaments unearthed from a huge box in the attic, laid out the wooden nativity scene she picked up somewhere on her travels, and spent a full day frantically rushing around the kitchen with pans of veg and jugs of gravy, her steamed-up glasses shoved on top of her head.

For a long time after Mum's death, I proclaimed that I hated Christmas, but it was more complex than that. Eventually, I realised that what I hated was accepting that I'd never be able to have the same Christmas without her. The day also coincides with when we found out she was going to die, so 25 December feels like a pivotal moment every year: the exact time my world changed forever. Part of me still wants to ignore the occasion and behave like it's any other day – but another part of me wants nothing more than to recreate exactly what I'd have done if Mum was still here.

Person-specific triggers

Person-specific triggers are usually sensory and always unique. They burrow deep into your memory bank, and old forgotten moments of your life are suddenly made vivid. Everything can remind you of the person you've lost: seeing strangers who look like them, noticing objects related to them, and going to physical spaces where you have memories of them. I still sometimes take the bus past the hospital where they were both treated, and I still can't look up to the sixth floor where Mum stayed.

Recently I realised I hadn't walked through a particular area of south London for a full decade, ever since Mum died. I don't know if I subconsciously made that decision, but I felt a lot of emotion rising up as I walked past the church hall where she used to take me for ballet classes, past the toyshop she used to work in and past the Pizza Express which always ended up being our "dinner out" spot. I glanced in the window of the Italian deli where she used to buy little tubs of fresh pesto for our dinner, and knew that the homemade sauce would always remind me of her. There are so many meals my parents used to cook: Dad's signature dishes like beef bourguignon, apple crumble, and chilli con carne with a packet of Cool Original Doritos; Mum's impeccable lasagne made with sheets of green pasta, and chicken "with a thousand pieces of garlic". Whenever I see these dishes on restaurant menus it gives me a little pang of nostalgia.

I sometimes think I hear their voices. My dad calling for our cat, or the way my mum would shout my name, sharp and high-pitched. There are acutely familiar noises too: the scraping sound of the key in the lock, or the creaking floorboards on the stairs.

Whenever I see their possessions in the normal world it jars me a little. Dad drove a common make of Nissan car and it's often parked in nearby streets. I see Mum's brand of makeup on the shelves: pale green compacts of Clinique powder and gold cylinders of

Touche Éclat. I see the kind of jewellery I would have bought for her, and the silly joke presents I would've given Dad for Christmas.

But the strangest feeling is when I actually "see" them. Before Dad died I spent a month walking the Camino de Santiago route through Spain. When I stopped at a bar for a coffee one morning, I saw a man I could have sworn was my dad. He had the same outfit, same stance, same hair, same glasses. It was an amazing coincidence at first, but then I felt a sense of foreboding and had to phone home to check that Dad was all right!

Unpredictable triggers

The triggers which upset me the most are the ones I can never predict. Dad's ironing basket has sat behind the kitchen door for over two years. I've half-started emptying it a dozen times, but I always come up short against the folded tea towels I used to buy him on my travels abroad; his perfectly square handkerchiefs with neatly stitched borders; the sets of matching cotton napkins we barely ever used. I pull the basket out from its "as-long-as-I-can-remember" spot behind the door, telling myself that this time I'll actually put the things away and get rid of the basket. I'm from a generation that doesn't care about the ironing – so I definitely don't need the damn basket – but every time I get halfway through the pile I already know I can't do it. It's too much. Someday in the future I'll be able to, but not yet.

The ironing basket is one of those triggers whose effect on me doesn't lessen. There are plenty of seemingly mundane situations that contain the same power, and it makes me scared of the everyday world. You can't prepare for these triggers – but there are still a few things you can do to lessen the impact they make on you.

Keep track of your triggers by making a list

It can be painful at first, but once you're aware of what they look like for you – and what emotions they bring up – it helps to identify what's dangerous for your emotional state, and makes it clear to you that not everything reminds you of death, grief, or the person you've lost. It also makes it easier to explain to loved ones what might set you off, and when they should keep a close eye on how you're doing.

Devise your coping strategies

When a trigger hits, know your fail-safe solutions. It might be phoning a particular person. It might be locking yourself in the bathroom for a bit of privacy. It might be playing Candy Crush until the feelings have dissipated a bit. I've realised that telling friends about what triggers me most has led to them pre-empting when I need help. Now I spend Christmas with my surrogate family and Easter with my best friend, all because I finally admitted how much I missed celebrating those occasions.

Don't be afraid of the triggers

I know they can be upsetting, but try not to avoid the triggers too much. When something reminds you of the person you've lost, it's understandable that you'll feel sad or scared or overwhelmed – but you won't always feel like that. The aim is to reach a point where the positive memories associated with triggers outweigh the negative ones, but this can only happen if you face up to the emotions and feel your way through them. It's a form of conditioning: familiarity prompts understanding and gives you an increased tolerance of how these triggers catch you out. Eventually, you'll appreciate them because they remind you of the person you lost and bring you closer to them again. A decade later, most of the triggers about my mum give me a little smile instead of twisting my stomach. Every time it happens, it makes me grateful I haven't forgotten her.

PART THREE

–

COMPLICATED GRIEF

9

When It All Gets Too Much

During the first few months after Dad's death, I was pretty numb. By month five or six I genuinely thought I was doing a bit better. My grief seemed to have settled into something of a pattern: I'd endure a few days of near-constant sobbing, until the emotion receded for a week or so. I thought the gaps between these tear-filled days would get longer, until eventually the intense grief would fade into memory.

I was so very wrong.

Amid a hot London summer, ten months after my dad's death, I sat in bed with the curtains closed for the third day running. My eyes ached. My chest felt hot and sticky with tears as it rose and fell rapidly. I looked at the laptop screen in front of me. This is what I wrote:

It's been two days of sobbing. I feel like I'm living on an edge: a windowsill, a roadside, a cliff. A place where others don't go. A place where I'm ignored, unloved, not valued. Not enough. I feel forgotten. I feel as if you're gifted with a handful of hearts who put you first, always, every day, no matter what – and I've lost mine. They've both gone.

And the pain of crying is so much, so huge, so everything, that I can't imagine how it'll ever change. I can't see myself ever being less depressed than this. Thirty years of life and I can't see a world where I don't hurt this much; when I'm not this damaged, this filled with pain, this overcome with constant sadness and constant, unending loneliness. I am alone. Always. No matter who says they care, I know they ultimately don't. Not like they did. Not like she did.

I don't know what I want, and I don't know what to do, and I don't know how to fix this. I've thought about suicide but I don't want to kill myself. I couldn't. They'd be so disappointed and sad that I couldn't make it through. But equally, I can't stand being so unhappy. I feel so unbelievably alone. I'm utterly exhausted. I can't see joy or positivity in anything the way I used to – even the tiniest possible moments of happiness are quashed almost immediately with my hollow grief instead. I miss them both so much it's like a physical level of loss. My body and mind have been through so much trauma that I can't begin to see how to repair that damage. And I can't bear how much it would have hurt Mum to know this is happening. I can't imagine how distraught she'd be: not disappointed, but just unbearably sad that this is how losing them has left me.

Mum's death didn't break me. Dad's death did. Suddenly I couldn't imagine being in any kind of sane world again. I didn't trust myself in the slightest. It felt like my stitches were coming loose, like my insides were falling out, like I had lost the structure and framework which held me upright.

I couldn't keep track of the simplest things. I couldn't retain any information. I couldn't focus on anything for longer than a few moments. I couldn't wake up in the mornings, but I couldn't get to sleep at night, so I panicked constantly about my sleep schedule. My boyfriend liked to drift off while the radio played, but I found myself lying in bed panicking, my heart rate rising because the sound of someone else speaking felt as if it were drilling directly into my head. I could *not* switch off, or relax, or calm down. I was on constant high alert.

I'd never felt more disconnected from everyone around me. I felt nobody understood what I was dealing with. Nobody seemed to recognise the enormity of my loss. Nobody seemed to recognise quite how seriously I was falling apart, and how desperately I needed someone to save me.

I didn't recognise myself. I was stunned by myself. I couldn't comprehend that this constant fever-dream of heightened emotion was now my life. I was terrified that it would last forever.

To put it simply, it felt like I had lost my mind.

Grieving feels like you're going crazy (for a reason!)

Looking back, I was probably suffering from a combination of post-traumatic stress disorder (PTSD), intense grief, severe depression and crippling anxiety throughout most of the first year after Dad's death. It was an overwhelming combination of mental health difficulties all swooping down at the same time. Nothing had prepared me for that level of intense emotion, so it felt like nothing I attempted could possibly drag me out.

But the cold hard truth is that grieving really does feel like you're going crazy. Why? Because the world you're currently inhabiting *is* crazy! Your life has been broken apart, and the process of putting it back together takes a ton of work. It's hard and it's brutal and it hurts like hell. Grief is suffering. There's no way to avoid that fact. Your body and your brain have had their foundations rocked, and it takes time for them to settle again.

Here is what nobody says about grief

The collective impression of grief seems to be passive. It's crying and sadness, feeling vulnerable and despondent, needing your friends to rally around you. It's rare to hear people talk about the volatility or genuine fire or utter madness that seems to envelop you in the depths of grief.

Nobody told me I'd feel fury coursing through my veins and I'd visualise myself punching total strangers so hard that they bled.

Nobody told me I'd slap myself repeatedly in the head while sobbing my eyes out in bed at 2 p.m. for reasons I couldn't fathom.

Nobody told me I could cry so hard I'd almost vomit from the sheer force of the roiling muscles in my chest.

Nobody told me grief could make me actually consider the possibility of suicide for the first time in my life, just to stop FEELING SO DAMN MUCH.

Does this sound crazy? If your answer is *yes*, just imagine these feelings underlying everything you do, and tell me whether you'd think you were going mad too.

It feels like the grief is getting worse, not better

This onslaught of emotion can be particularly terrifying if you think you've been making progress. Perhaps the first few months of grief were seriously hard but then the pressure eased a bit. Perhaps you've been able to enjoy yourself with friends more often recently. Perhaps there have been days, or even entire weeks, when death wasn't at the forefront of your mind. And then it's all gone to absolute shit again.

Indicators that it's really getting too much

You probably already know your grief is getting too much to handle by yourself. The knowledge is deep in your core: a heavy sullen weight which is a constant reminder of how damaged and broken you feel.

Your behaviour has started to change. You might pull away completely from your support system – constantly shouting at your partner, refusing help from your friends, always choosing to be alone instead of with people. The reason you're doing this might feel completely confused, or it might feel something like this:

You're terrified of losing anyone else you love, or who

loves you, so it's easier to push them away and save yourself even more pain.

You feel so vulnerable that any hint of people not "understanding" what's happening to you is just another reminder that the one person who *did* understand has now disappeared from your life forever.

You feel you don't deserve someone else caring about you. Because look what happens when someone does care. They end up dying, and who's to say if that's something to do with you?

You wonder whether all this is punishment for something you did, and dragging anyone else in is just going to result in more hurt.

You wonder if you're destined to be alone. What's the point in pretending? Everyone's going to die and leave you at some point – it might as well be now. Better get used to it fast and then you'll be ready the next time – because you know for certain that there'll always be a next time.

You almost want to be cruel and uncaring to the people who love you. You're horribly tempted to see what happens if you push them so hard that they throw up their hands and say, "I've had enough" – because then you'll feel validated in the knowledge that you're unfixable, intolerable, and grief has well and truly fucked your life up.

These horrible, harmful, self-damaging thought processes are actually just defence mechanisms. They're our body's way of protecting ourselves from suffering any further trauma. They're bizarrely rooted in self-preservation, even if it doesn't sound like it – but if we allow these defences to get their way, they can inflict so much more damage.

All these thoughts have spun their way through my head. They've often had the power to make all my decisions for me and dictate how I behave. And for a long time I let them, because I was terrified of allowing myself to even contemplate being happy. I didn't think it was safe.

Actually, it was bigger than that: I thought being happy was STUPID.

Death makes the world seem cruel, and you lose all trust in it

When someone dies it can turn your concept of the

world upside down. I've never been so suspicious and distrustful of my environment than in the months after my dad's death. I'd grown up thinking that the worst thing I could experience was my parents dying – and it had happened. So there seemed no reason why I shouldn't assume every other terrifying and awful thing could also happen to me. If both my parents could die, I could just as easily die in a plane crash, or find myself in a terrorist attack, or get hit by a car, or be killed by someone breaking into my house. This is a classic symptom of anxiety, and once you begin thinking like this it's hard to stop.

Even if I occasionally felt somewhat happy or OK, an unavoidable truth always wormed its way back into my mind.

My parents are DEAD! How am I ever supposed to ignore that fact? How can I possibly build a positive life when that reality sits at the centre of everything I do, everything I am, everything I have the potential to become?

The irony is knowing how upset your parents would be to see you so sad about their deaths. I know Mum would feel so awful that she was indirectly responsible for my depression and anxiety – and she's also the person I want to speak to about all this! And I can't!

Reaching the rock bottom of grief

Most of us have a rock-bottom moment in our grief. Frustratingly, it's something which is usually only identifiable afterwards, once you've begun to heal.

My worst point in the grieving process happened in October 2018, as the first anniversary of my dad's death approached. For months I felt as if I were stumbling through a thick haze of fog, completely unable to smile or speak and feeling totally empty and emotionless. Nothing seemed to lift my mood. The tiniest thing felt completely overwhelming. I couldn't bear to be touched, I felt constantly suffocated, and all I wanted was to be left alone. If it had been possible, I'd have slept my way through those months. At that moment I honestly thought I'd never get over the grief. I thought my life as I'd known it was over.

I seriously needed help, and thankfully I found it. I spent an intensive week with a Cognitive Behavioural Therapist (CBT), talking through these overwhelming emotions and navigating a new way through them until I began to settle into a less pressurised state.

My biggest realisation at this point was that I simply could not battle through my grief alone – but that I needed to choose the right people and resources to help me through it.

10

Helping Yourself Through Grief

There's something extremely frustrating about the timeline of grief. Those of us who experienced it a while ago recognise that time is, annoyingly, the clichéd healer we've all heard about. But when you're in the thick of it, floored by the lack of the person you've lost, you're convinced that everyone else is wrong. Nothing can change this certainty you feel, deep down in your gut: life as you knew it is over, and there'll be nothing positive again.

If I tell you the positive parts of your life will come back eventually, you won't believe me. But right now, when it still feels fresh, there are still some things you *can* do to change how your grief feels.

I know that might sound scary. You feel so vulnerable that the idea of being your own salvation makes no sense.

But I'll let you in on a secret: grief has made me so damn strong.

Think about it. I've watched two people I loved die, and I'm still here. I've lost my entire family and I'm still here. I've weathered ten years of intense emotional trauma and yes, you guessed it, I'm still here.

But it's taken a long time to realise this. And it doesn't negate the enormity of what I've lost, either. Often, in my sadder moments, I still feel like my world is over, and that I'll always be in pain. That's because grief is no joke. Even in its most passive state, it's seriously hard, tough, difficult, and treacherous. But grief is also an active process. It's an action which I and millions of others do every single hour, every single day. Recognising the part you can play in your own grief process can be a really empowering thing.

When grief becomes an action

A lot of self-work comes with grieving. You have to let go of what you thought your life might look like. You have to learn how to be a new version of yourself without the person you've lost. It takes bravery. It takes time.

For a long while, I felt grief was an overwhelmingly passive thing. Grief was happening to me, in spite of me, lying on my chest like a heavy woollen weight. If clouds had stones in them, that's what it felt like.

But as time goes on, grief begins to re-form. It becomes a new entity. It becomes an action. Somehow you start to "do your grief" – and that means you also begin to take ownership of it. That's a significant progression.

So how do we begin to "action" our grief? What do we need to do?

Accept that being alone and feeling lonely is always a possibility – but it doesn't have to be your permanent state

Feeling completely alone is one of the hardest parts of grief I've had to manoeuvre myself through. It's the major reason why I decided to write this book – because the original blog article I wrote about dealing with the deaths of my parents has led to hundreds of people sending me their own stories of grief, and thanking me for making them feel a bit less alone.

I've learned that so many of us are searching for a parallel experience of grief because we somehow find comfort in knowing that our emotional, vulnerable, terrifying situation has happened to someone else. And

I promise you, it has. No matter how unlikely it feels, there's someone else out there who has no siblings and lost their mum when they were twenty and their dad when they were twenty-nine. I've been messaged by at least three people whose grief stories match mine – and they're just the ones who speak English and managed to find my article!

Accepting the possibility of loneliness at times in your life is a big step to wading through grief. When you're willing to entertain that possibility, you're able to see that it's not a constant – and that you're also allowed to do something about it. At one of my most lonely moments, I wrote this in my diary:

I am so scared of being alone. I am scared of being alone forever. I am scared of daring to live my life properly again because it might confirm to me that I am, actually, alone. I am scared I'll never find someone to understand me the way I crave to be understood, to love me the way I want to be loved, to care and support me the way I need to be cared for and supported. I am scared nobody will ever put me first again. I am scared I've failed my life already. I am scared I've failed Mum and Dad. I am scared I'm failing them right now. I am scared they wouldn't be able to find pride in how I live now, but I'm too exhausted and scared and raw to do anything other than what I'm doing. I am scared my life is never going to get any better.

When I look at this now, I think it boils down to one thing. I was scared that I'd never feel happy in the same way that I did when my parents were alive.

I was equating loneliness with a lack of being understood and loved in the specific ways my parents used to understand and love me.

But just because those relationships are no longer "alive" doesn't mean they didn't happen. Any individual relationship you have with anyone is unique – so it stands to reason that nobody can understand the magnitude of that particular loss.

That lack of understanding is what's so difficult to adjust to. I often felt I didn't want people to know the depths of my grief. I was almost possessive of the pain, because it belonged wholly to the strength of connection I shared with my parents, and particularly my mum. I was an only child, and Mum loved me with a wild abandon which occasionally bordered on obsessive. She lavished so much attention on me that in my early teens, I felt smothered and suffocated by it! But when she died it felt as if a tap which had been flowing at full power throughout my life had suddenly and inexplicably been turned off. My dad loved me in his own way, but never with the same ferocity, the same dramatic obviousness as Mum's love – and I will miss trusting a love which felt as obvious as breathing for the rest of my life.

But just because that specific form of love has vanished from your life doesn't mean you're not loved. Soon after Dad's death, my best friend hugged me outside a train station and said, "None of us can know what you're going through. And that's OK. But we're here to help any way we possibly can." Hearing her honesty meant so much, and it's always stuck with me as a result. I think it's important not to try and cling on to the thought that someone "gets it", because we know ultimately they can't, and that's what makes us so sad and lonely. Despite all the people who want to help you, you have to journey through your grief alone. But you can still ask others to stand beside you while you're going through it.

Identify the people in your support system, and ask them for help when you need it

A good support network is invaluable in any recovery process. I feel acutely vulnerable with no parents, and sometimes I worry that my friends can never replicate the love my parents gave me. I can also get anxious that I'm bothering them with my constant life updates! But they're my friends for a reason. They know and love me in a different way from my parents. They're able to share the emotional weight of supporting me, and they can buoy me up in ways I don't expect. In the first months after my dad's death, they were able to help with the unforeseen admin that pops up: unexpected phone calls from that one distant relative you forgot to tell who's devastated they missed the funeral, or the car insurance company who claim they're still owed money and demand to speak to your late father.

However, some people aren't sure whether you need their help. If these friends and family somehow aren't aware that you regard them as part of your support system, tell them! You might think you're being clear about who you expect support from, but often people are unsure of what's expected of them. Now is the time to be vocal and demanding when you need help – but it can be difficult.

At heart, I'm a very proud person (much like my dad!). Although I can easily talk about grief and what I'm feeling in a general sense, I still find it extremely difficult to ask for help when I need it most. Perhaps I don't want to disappoint the people who think I'm "doing better" with my grief, or perhaps it stems from an innate fear that what I ask for – what I make myself vulnerable for – won't be provided. It can feel like one heartbreak too many to ask someone for help and be

denied. Much easier to just not ask, right?
Unfortunately, that leaves me feeling even more alone,
and even more overwhelmed.

It might feel way too stressful and exhausting to
explain what specific help you need in grief, but when
the potential outcome is support and relief, I promise
you it's worth it.

Choose your surrogate family

When you're grieving, you're often told to "surround
yourself with the people that love you." For a long
time, I abjectly refused to see this as a positive. Instead,
I repeatedly told myself that nobody loved me like
Mum did: nobody ever could, because nobody had
known me so intensely and so long. My mum was my
constant champion, and it was very hard to
comprehend the idea that anyone else would take on a
similar role in my life. Mum was almost obliged to be
that person for me, surely, because she gave birth to
me – so why would anyone else choose it?

There's a hell of a lot of self-sabotage in this thought
process. A big lack of self-esteem and self-worth. Of
course other people love you! It may not be in the exact
way that your parents did, but that doesn't mean it's
any less valuable. Over time you start to notice all the
loving ways that your friends care for you, and you

begin to construct a new family for yourself. My closest friends know every detail about me, especially the things I would usually have told my parents about first. My successes, my upsets, the things I need someone to get excited about with me and the things I need support with: they're the ones to receive my texts and phone calls.

When it comes to special occasions which would have been spent with family – Christmas, Easter, even Mother's Day and Father's Day – I'm with my friends and their families instead. I used to dread these occasions and tried my best to ignore them, along with the emotions they brought up and the memories of how my parents would have behaved during them. It's taken me a while to admit to both myself and others that what I really wanted was to be surrounded by the people who love me and make me happy, even if those people can't be my parents anymore.

Talk to a doctor

Your support system of friends and family is particularly important when it comes to getting professional help. Like most people, I was so engulfed by my grief that it took a close friend saying, "Flora, you're depressed and you need to speak to a doctor," for me to finally realise she was right.

Unfortunately, that doctor's appointment didn't help me much. It was about eight months after Dad's death, when I'd hit a seriously low point in my grieving journey: I'd barely been sleeping, I couldn't stop crying and I felt as close to suicidal as I ever had. During the five-minute appointment (all that's available for a one-off appointment with the NHS), I said I was having trouble sleeping and that my dad had died recently. In return, the doctor immediately gave me one prescription for sleeping pills and another for antidepressants. She had no time to explain what taking the antidepressants would entail – what mood swings they might give me, how long they'd take to kick in, what side-effects there could be, how long I'd need to stay on them, how long it would take to wean myself off them eventually. Nothing. The doctor spent longer warning me about the sleeping pills because they were renowned for being addictive.

I left the doctor's office feeling confused and apprehensive about taking antidepressants. I began to research the brand of pills she'd given me, and it seemed they could make your symptoms and difficult emotions worse for the first few weeks – and then when you wanted to come off them it could induce another huge emotional shake-up.

Everyone's decisions surrounding antidepressants for their mental health and/or grief are completely valid, but my eventual decision came down to a gut feeling. I was resolute that grief was something I needed to actively feel my way through. I knew how long I'd buried my emotions about my mum's death, and it had resulted in a breakdown seven years later. So after my dad's death, I wanted to face the grief head-on without medication.

Talk to a therapist or counsellor – but only when you feel ready

Not everyone needs therapy – plenty of people get through awful situations without professional help – but I still think everyone can benefit from talking to a therapist. It doesn't work if you're pushed into therapy by someone else, though. It has to be a realisation you come to yourself. And even when you've decided that therapy is the way to go, it can still be tricky finding the right person to speak to.

A month after Mum's death, my university assigned me a bereavement counsellor. It didn't go well. I entered the tiny room feeling relatively fine, spent an hour with a woman who purposefully asked questions which made me cry, and then I left in floods of tears. Walking back to my house in an emotional state I didn't need to be in felt unnecessary and hurtful, so I went for two more sessions and then never returned.

Perhaps the university counsellor just wasn't a good fit. Even so, I know now that I wasn't ready to speak about Mum or how her death had affected me. I hadn't even absorbed the gravity of the situation at that point.

It took me seven years of trying to navigate grief on my own before I truly realised I needed therapy. It happened when I was watching a YouTuber vlogging about her mental health. She said, "If you feel bad about yourself, you should speak to someone." It was such a simple statement, yet it totally floored me. I did feel bad about myself! Most of the time, in fact. I was constantly angry at myself, chastising myself for the way I behaved or over-thought or underachieved. I was hypercritical of what I perceived as my flaws and failures. I was becoming increasingly anxious about the unknowns of the world, to the extent that it took me significant time to even leave the house. I was sad more often than I was happy. And yet for some reason, I'd never considered that all these feelings might warrant going to therapy. I was still in a mindset which said: "Mum died seven years ago, long enough to mean that I'm fine with her death now. All these thoughts and feelings are just who I am, and I should be able to sort them out myself." The worst internal thought of all was that perhaps I was just destined to be an unhappy person. Perhaps I just had to accept that truth, and deal with it.

Watching that YouTube video spurred me into action. As soon as I realised that my mental health was suffering significantly, it was as if a floodgate had opened. Suddenly I was in desperate need of someone to speak to, and I instinctively chose the first therapist who responded to my emails. She wasn't the warmest of people and I didn't feel an immediate connection with her, but my need for help overruled any slight misgivings. After just a few weekly sessions my dad went into hospital, so our therapy conversations switched from discussing my life to discussing how I'd cope with Dad's impending death. At that point, I couldn't imagine explaining my whole backstory to a different therapist, so I stuck with her.

In the last two years since Dad's death, I've tried out a few different therapists and I've finally found "my person", a specialist in CBT. We have an easy and positive connection: she makes jokes, we laugh, we chat naturally, and I don't feel on edge around her. Every session reveals something new and helps me gain clarity on coping with my grief and anxiety. Speaking with her makes me feel stronger, and more capable.

If you decide to find a therapist and then don't feel they're quite right for you, please remember it's OK to try different people. It can feel difficult to tell someone you don't get on with them enough to continue working together, but it's their job and they'll understand.

What can help is having a few things straight in your mind first:

- ◦ What would you like to get out of therapy?
- ◦ What main topics are you hoping to talk about?
- ◦ What kind of therapist are you looking for?
- ◦ Male or female?
- ◦ Young or old?
- ◦ Someone who practices talking therapy or CBT?

Remember, as someone suffering from a bereavement, you already have a "free pass" for needing therapy. It doesn't matter how long ago you suffered that bereavement. It's always going to affect you in some way, so it's always appropriate for you to talk about that death with a therapist.

Write down your feelings, and your memories of them

Writing is one of the most powerful tools we can use to process our thoughts. It's a form of release, a catharsis. Write letters to the person you've lost. Write the way they made you feel. Write the emotions you're feeling right now. Write a list of what makes you happy. Write a stream of consciousness with swear words and slang words and spelling mistakes. Write the same meditative phrase two dozen times in increasingly messy handwriting if that feels right to you. Tear holes in the page with the tip of the biro and get some feelings out that way.

I type my mind out onto a laptop screen most days: just a few sentences if that's all I have to say, but sometimes it's more. Sometimes it's unintended essays of feeling, letters streaming from my fingers and my eyes skittering over the words without reading them. I don't often look back, as it's the act of transference – getting thoughts out of my head and onto a page instead – which makes me feel cleaner afterwards.

When I learned my mum was dying, I opened a new document on my laptop and started writing down the details of what was happening. I still don't know what gave me that urge – whether it was in case I forgot, or whether it helped me make sense of such a surreal situation – but it felt entirely necessary to do it.

When Dad was diagnosed as terminal, I began to do the same thing. Every day, while I crisscrossed London on the train, I scribbled in a notebook. All the things I couldn't find the words for out loud became much easier to say in writing. And in the first days after he died, when I suddenly panicked that I'd forget all the little quirks which made him who he was, I opened a new Word document called "Dad memories".

I wrote down the pet names he used to call me, the in-jokes we shared, the way he moved, the familiar phrases he always said – and whenever another memory pops into my head I still add it to the list.

Look at photos and videos of them

My mum was obsessed with taking photos, so my house is full of photo albums, framed photos, loose wallets with extra photos and even a plastic box filled with her "unwanted" photos – which she apparently still had to keep! Her love of photography used to frustrate me as a teenager but now I'm grateful, as it's meant I've been able to replace the familiar framed photos around the house with different, "new" images of my family.

A few years after Mum's death, I became convinced I'd forgotten the sound of her voice. Then my dad unearthed all the home videos she'd recorded – the majority of my childhood caught on tape, with occasional glimpses of her curly hair and happy smile amongst footage of my ballet classes, birthday parties and Christmas celebrations. Dad transferred hundreds of hours of that footage onto DVD before he died, so now I'm able to hear my parents' voices, see them move, and even see how they interacted with me as a child.

Add them back into your daily life - talk to them and talk about them

I'm not sure when it started, but whenever I see double numbers I say hello to my mum. Out loud. It happens pretty often, especially when I glance at my phone screen to see 17:17 or 21:21. It always makes me smile – and it means there are multiple moments each day when she's in my mind. For Dad, it's daffodils and robins. Each spring I find myself saying hi to him more often, thanks to the sudden bursts of yellow flowers in public parks and on grass verges – but there's also a pair of robins living in my garden, so whenever I spot them I think of Dad.

Establishing these regular reminders of my parents has been so cathartic that it almost fills the space where I would text or phone them for a chat. And if these passive reminders don't feel enough, I speak to them out loud. It felt a bit bizarre at first but I've grown to find it normal now, and it's comforting to imagine their reactions to the things I say. I know they're not really there – but it's nice to imagine that they're behind me, beside me, or just out of sight.

Speaking about them is important too – and it doesn't need to be in the context of death. I still tell funny stories about them all the time. One of my recent favourites is telling my friends in the travel blogging community that I'm almost certain my mum would have started her own travel blog so that she could befriend them, keep tabs on what they were up to, and generally try to get as involved as possible with that side of my life. It makes people laugh and say they wish they'd met her – which in turn makes me so happy, and proud of her, and sad for both of us. But it's all right – she's still part of my life in that way. I'm letting it happen. I'm choosing to bring her into my present.

It's wonderful when you realise that you get to choose how vividly your parents live on. I make sure I use the same strange theatrical words and obscure phrases they did, then explain the context and tell my friends that I want those phrases to carry on existing, despite the fact their users are no longer here. I actively try to keep my parents in the conversation, because talking about them keeps them alive.

Give yourself permission to be happy – remember what it feels like

One day I was listening to an episode of a podcast called *The Griefcast*, and the man being interviewed said he'd once been asked about the happiest day of his life. As he described the memory of a perfect day with his family before his brother had died, I started to cry in the middle of the street – because I honestly couldn't think of my happiest day. Nothing sprang into my mind.

I felt sad for myself, because in that moment I knew I'd been trying so damn hard to protect myself from pain that I wasn't allowing anything positive into my life either.

Pretty quickly afterwards, I made the conscious decision to allow myself occasional moments of happiness, instead of shutting them down as soon as they bubbled up inside me. I gave myself permission to be happy – something I hadn't realised I was able to do.

After a trauma, your fight or flight response is so heightened that your subconscious tells you relaxing into any state other than high alert is stupid. If you relax, you're vulnerable – and that means you're open to the possibility of being hurt again. But you *are* allowed to feel better. It's not an insult to the person you've lost to continue enjoying your life without them. So give yourself permission to be happy! Recognise what the sensation of being happy feels like! Take joy in those moments, and remember that this was once a familiar feeling for you in the past, even if it's not so common right now.

Be patient and don't pressure yourself - grieving takes time

Grief is unique. It happens in its own time, but most of us aren't prepared to wait it out. We look for quick fixes and surefire solutions. We assume it *can* be fixed. But in fact, there's only one way to deal with this loss, this pain, this constant threat of crying: we have to feel our way through it. Face it. Handle it. Be deep within it. I know it's scary, but it *will* get better eventually.

11

Feeling Lighter

One day in early spring, over a year after Dad's death, I
bought five bunches of daffodils for a pound each.
When I got home and divided them up into vases, I
took one upstairs to put on the chest of drawers
opposite my bed and realised, finally, just how messy
and overstuffed with photos it was. The surface was
thick with dust. So I stacked up the photos I didn't
want there any more (so many of me as a beaming
toddler!) and picked up a little square dish Dad had
left there, filled with pens, rubbers, coins, a compass, a
pebble, a box of thin matches. Classic Dad stuff. I
cleared half the detritus so I could wipe away the dust,
and suddenly the room changed. I looked around and
knew I'd released an invisible weight.

One night that autumn, I left the heating on until 11

p.m., but when I went into the kitchen it was still chilly. I decided I should copy the new neighbours in the house opposite, who'd drawn their kitchen curtains tight. I started tugging on my own curtains, which I don't think were ever closed when my parents were alive. I willed them to travel around the rail without ripping their linings or spewing decades of dust. They more or less closed, and I tucked them above the radiator. And the next morning, even with a smattering of snow on the ground outside, the kitchen didn't feel quite as cold as before.

When you cry, it doesn't last as long as it used to. You aren't floored by it, and you don't need to spend the rest of the day in bed. When you think about them, or imagine you hear their voices, or see something which reminds you of them, it doesn't fill you with despair and sadness. It feels bittersweet instead; there's a pang of loss, but it's not completely awful any more. It might make you sigh a little, but it's manageable.

You begin to realise that you're not the same as your parents

Losing your parents early in life often means you compare yourself to them. For a long time, I viewed most of my personality traits as stemming either from Mum or from Dad – almost as if I didn't have the ability or choice to be my own person. Mum was a born socialiser and could make friends anywhere, whereas Dad liked his privacy and often chose a night at home over all the social invitations my mum tried to entice him into. Of course, I ended up being a mix of the two: a self-described extroverted introvert, who loves being around people and thrives in social environments but needs to recharge with time alone. Eventually, I realised that it doesn't matter whether I'm more like my mum or my dad; it doesn't mean I was any less close to them just because I'm not their carbon copy.

When you do recognise elements of them in yourself, it's happy, not sad. Sometimes I catch a glimpse of my mum's expression when I look in the mirror. Recently I saw a photo of my dad and me together and realised how alike our face shapes are. Were. It happens with habits too, and turns of phrase – and every time I notice, it feels lovely, not painful. I remember when it used to hurt like hell, but enough time has passed for it to be OK now.

You think of them as a real person who had flaws

For a long time, I thought of Mum as a perfect person who I'd lost. Except of course she wasn't perfect. She was a normal person with flaws and weaknesses, just like anyone else, and she often used to drive me crazy! During my teenage years, it would set my teeth on edge when she sang along with the radio a beat behind the rhythm. I'd roll my eyes and grimace when she insisted on taking photos of me at every opportunity. I have a distinct memory of hating how loudly she breathed when we watched TV together. And yet for years after her death, I refused to remember any of her flaws. It felt sacrilegious to admit she could ever have done anything wrong.

Putting my mum on a pedestal put a lot of pressure on me. I was forcing myself to mourn someone who didn't actually exist, and making myself feel guilty for not appreciating her when she was alive. I think the speed of her death contributed to my guilt too. By the time Dad died, I had come to terms with our complex relationship, and I haven't airbrushed any memories since his death.

Once you see your parent as a real person instead of an idealised version, it's easier to remember the less positive parts of them – which in turn makes the grieving process just a little easier.

You realise they're still "kind of here"

Somehow their presence in your life seems to grow

bigger. Even if they're not physically here, they're still in your mind – and you begin to instinctively know what they'd have said in a particular situation, or how they'd have reacted.

One day I was out walking with a close friend when I had an acute awareness of just how much my mum would've liked her. It didn't matter that they'd never had the chance to meet. Somehow, the very fact that I knew they'd have got on ("like a house on fire", as Mum would say!) was almost as good. And when I feel like I need support from my parents, I visualise a little cheer squad: my mum, over-excited and extremely loud with flamboyant hand gestures everywhere, and my dad beside her, perhaps looking a little uncomfortable but grinning nonetheless. It gives me the feeling that I'm living my life for the three of us, instead of just for myself.

Only you know your grief – so you can't be doing it wrong

There is no right, wrong, recommended or ill-advised way to grieve. There can't be, because every single grief process is unique. Many people reading this may think my advice isn't appropriate for them at all!

It's so easy to pressurise yourself into thinking, "I should have dealt with this by now." That's a normal feeling. Try to remember that grief doesn't have an end point. It doesn't just finish. There isn't an expiry date.

Much as I wish I could tell you that one day I woke up and was fully over Mum's death, you and I both know that's just not possible. What does seem to happen, though, is the gradual lessening of grief. Even though I still have those lightning-bolt moments when I gasp, "They died. THEY DIED?" and the world feels suddenly surreal, those moments don't last as long as they once did.

My biggest realisation, through the aftermath of two deaths, is that I needed to listen to my body. Be aware of what you truly feel you need, and follow that internal wisdom. Don't let anyone tell you it's been "long enough"'or you "should be better by now." This is your journey, and nobody needs to understand it but you. Guard it fiercely, and experience that journey for yourself.

Your grief is not who you are

Please try to not let your grief define you. I've struggled with this ever since my mum died, and doubly so now that Dad's gone too. Irrespective of this terrible loss you've suffered, you are still your own person. **Grief may have happened to you, but it doesn't make you who you are.** In fact, these losses might shape you into a better, stronger version of yourself.

If Mum hadn't died when I was twenty, I would have made such different choices in life that I can't imagine what I'd be like now. But because she did die, I became a traveller. I became a writer. I became fiercely protective of my friends and anyone I know who's dealing with loss. I became passionate about expressing my feelings and investigating why I feel the way I do.

It's taken a long time for me to realise that I have a choice. I don't have to self-identify as an orphan, or a griever, or the girl who lost her parents. I can re-establish my identity without them. I may have lost the safety net of these two stalwart supporters in my life, but that loss has also given me a strange gift: the drive to become my own supporter and to learn how to fill that same supportive role for others in my life.

Moreover, I know deep down that both my beautiful, hilarious, ever-loving parents would hate their deaths to affect me so negatively. And that gives me the push to keep moving forward.

You get to dictate how the rest of your life plays out

It's easy to feel alone when those who loved you most

are gone. But you're not. Their love still existed. You still knew them. I may be an adult orphan now – and you might be too – but we're still here. We're still living, fiercely and passionately, with every fibre of our being. We might sob occasionally because that's what grief does to us, but we're doing them proud.

We're living, in spite of our loss. We're living because of them, and because we loved them. That's all we need to do.

PART FOUR

–

THE LANGUAGE OF GRIEF

12

How to Help a Griever

If you're supporting someone through grief, this chapter is for you. It's wonderful that you want to help someone cope with this pain. And if you're the one who's grieving, feel free to show this chapter to someone who needs to read it!

They know you want to help. They know you're trying your best. But there's a grief-chasm which sits between you and them. No words will ever fix what they've gone through; no action can offer a real solution. And you should know that they aren't expecting anything you say or do to magically fix them, either!

So what can you offer? It might be simpler than you think. A bit of comfort. A bit of relief. The promise of compassion and companionship, should they need it, or maybe a bit of space to process this alone. You can help with the most mundane things – walking the dog, doing the hoovering, buying the groceries, cooking them something you know they like to eat.

Please don't ignore them – even if you're scared you'll upset them

When you learn they're grieving, you might think they want privacy and solitude. You might accidentally provoke them into getting upset, and you don't want to make them sad. Maybe it's just better to leave them to it. They'll reach out for help if they want it, right?

Wrong. Here's the shocker: they're thinking about the person they lost all the damn time. They're always in their heads (there truly hasn't been a day in ten years when I haven't thought about my mum). So it's good news for you – there's no way they'll resent you for bringing up the topic of their dead parent. I promise. What they might resent is if you push at a particular strand when they're not ready to talk about it.

In the simplest of terms? You're not going to make them "more upset". You're not going to remind them about the magnitude of what they've lost. They already know. So much loneliness comes with loss, and it makes support and companionship even more valuable. However clumsy your attempt to make them feel better might be, as long as it comes from a genuine place of care there's a likelihood they'll appreciate it!

And I guarantee that saying something "wrong" to them can never be as painful as saying nothing at all.

Acknowledge the reality of their pain - please don't try to sugarcoat it

It's human nature to look for positive solutions in bad situations. Unfortunately, this is one situation where putting on a brave face is counterproductive. There's nothing more infuriating (and, frankly, exhausting) than someone trying to put a positive spin on death, when the truth of the matter is that it's unequivocally shit.

Lines to avoid like the plague include:

- "They're in a better place."
- "They wouldn't want you to be sad."
- "At least it's over now."
- "At least it happened quickly."
- "At least they had a good life."

It's OK to say "I don't know what to say"

They don't mind! They're not judging you for not having the correct grief etiquette! Honestly, they're just grateful that you're here and that you want to help. If you're finding it awkward, or can't seem to express yourself, try saying something like:

"I'm really sorry if I *do* say something wrong – so please pull me up on it if that happens! I don't want to upset you any more than you have been, but I also want you to know I love you and will do what I can to support you."

It'll be a relief for you because you've admitted the difficulty of responding to someone else's grief. And it'll be a relief for them because it makes the support much more simple. You are *here*. That's what matters.

Be honest, truthful and real with them

Please don't rehash quotes you've heard in movies or read in books. There's a strong chance they've heard them multiple times – and they already hate them. "Sorry for your loss" always sounds weirdly artificial. Although they understand it's what everyone's been trained to say, it means much more if they can tell you're speaking from the heart.

If hearing about the death has reminded you of something good about that person, tell your friend the memory! Hearing positive stories about their parents is wonderful. It doesn't have to be a sad topic all the time. But if you do feel sad, shocked, angry, or like your breath has been knocked out of you? Tell them that.

Hearing a real reaction is such a relief.

Please don't compare your grief to theirs

Even if you've suffered the same kind of loss, it doesn't mean they want to hear about your coping strategies or how you're doing better now. Unless they specifically ask, don't impose your own handling of grief on them. Everyone copes with this differently. If they want to hear about your experiences, they'll ask.

If you ask them how they are, be prepared for an emotional response

At certain times in the grief journey, there can be a grim satisfaction in seeing people react awkwardly to something you've said. My internal monologue has often gone something like this:

Oh, so you're asking how I am? I can tell you don't really want to know but fuck it, I'm feeling wretched so here it comes – "Actually, I feel pretty awful. My dad's about to die and I can't stop crying and yet I'm standing in a pub pretending I'm fine, but of course I'm not, and life is pretty fucking horrendous." *– Oh, that's made you uncomfortable, has it? Well, this is what can happen when you bloody ask how people are!*

You've got to understand that their emotions are all over the place. It feels like all bets are off. They walk down the street and things look normal in the world, but actually this utterly surreal, bizarre thing is happening inside them:

My person is dying, they're literally dying. How can things possibly be normal in the world when they won't be in it next week or next month?

Occasionally this state gives them a surreal sense of freedom to do and say whatever they feel like. Being mired in grief doesn't feel like normal life. Grief is messy. It's unpredictable. It's wild and confusing and they often have no idea how they're going to behave or react until it's already happening. It can be really scary. They're not their rational selves. Please remember that.

If you're their closest support system, prepare to see a lot of conflicted emotion

Husbands, wives, long-term partners, siblings, closest friends: take note. They've chosen you to help them through this grief, and unfortunately, that means you'll see the darker side of it. They might get angry at you for seemingly no reason. They might refuse all care and contact. They might throw things. It might look like they hate you, but it's actually because you're the one person they know won't leave them when they flare up. Because you love them and they love you, they know they can let all the emotions out in your company – which might feel unfair on you!

From the outside, they may look the same – but their internal landscape has irrevocably shifted

The tiniest thing has the power to tip them over the edge. Stubbing a toe or breaking a plate can feel like the end of the world. It's because their world really *has* been changed forever by the loss they've experienced – but it probably doesn't look like it from the outside.

To help them, try to focus on the significance of the bereavement as a whole instead of the individual situations which make them upset. In their minds, they aren't separate moments. They're a fast-moving conveyor belt of stark reminders to prove the world is against them. Saying, "You're crying because you broke that plate? OK, let's fix the plate!" isn't the solution. Understand that for them, the plate is yet another thing that's broken and destroyed. What if this is always going to happen now? What if everything they care about is going to break, and what if they're powerless to stop it?

You need to recognise that the loss of their parents has profoundly changed their sense of who they are and how they behave from here onwards.

Listen to what they're saying without words

Do they want to be left alone? Do they want to watch TV for 24 hours straight and eat junk food in silence? Do they want to go for a day-long hike in the countryside? Do they want to spend the night in a bar downing shots? Do they just want a hug? Sometimes being tactile and close is enough. Then again, I went through phases where I suddenly couldn't bear close physical contact – perhaps because it wasn't coming from my parents, and so it felt like such an inadequate replacement.

Be active, not passive – offer them specific help

Please don't ask, "What can I do?" Please don't say, "Let me know if you need anything!" Grieving folks are usually exhausted, both mentally and physically. It's difficult for them to identify what they specifically need – and when they do think of something, it often feels too demanding or awkward to say, "Hey, can you do X and Y for me?" Just because they're dealing with grief doesn't mean they're suddenly competent at asking their friends to do things for them. Besides, there's the possibility that when they ask for help they might be refused. When they're grieving it's too painful to be let down by someone, so it's much easier to just not bother asking.

But when someone offers a specific form of help, it becomes so much easier to say yes. Offer to help with their daily activities – you could fill their fridge, walk their dog, or drive them to the supermarket. Offer to help with practical death admin tasks – you could call people to share the news of what's happened, give them the name of a good probate lawyer, or help to sort through potential charity shop donations. That said, only make the offer if you know that you can and will be able to fulfil it.

Don't be offended if they seem antisocial

This is the moment in your relationship where your offer to "be there" for them means putting them and their needs first. You might spend an hour journeying to their house and then not be welcomed inside. You might make plans with them and then they cancel at the last minute. You might feel annoyed, but please don't show them this reaction. Please be OK with their changeable behaviour. In fact, you can actively prepare for this possibility by reducing the pressure they might feel. Saying something like, "I'll be at this cafe / restaurant / bar at 7 p.m. on Tuesday. If you feel up to it, fantastic – I'll pay for lunch / dinner / drinks. But if you decide at the last minute you don't want to come, that's absolutely fine too. Whatever works for you." Whenever my friends said this before we were due to meet up, I felt a wave of relief wash over me – and felt very grateful that they understood how changeable my emotions could be.

Be aware that every grieving person is different

For some people, receiving flowers is a wonderful reminder that they're loved. For others, it's the worst possible thing. It means finding a clean vase, finding somewhere in the house to put them and then coping with dead, wilting flowers next week. In the same way, some people (myself included) feel a strong need to talk about what's happened, while others clam up for years and might even resent the pressure to talk from those around them.

It's also entirely changeable. At this point in my life, I'm usually comfortable talking about grief and death whenever the conversation arises, but there are still moments when I don't want to – and I don't necessarily know when those moments will occur. So don't push them too far if they're not ready.

Ask them what they need instead of assuming

You might feel they need privacy, but have you actually asked them? So many people have told me over the years that they didn't reach out when my parents died because they didn't want to intrude or burden me. It's understandable – but when you've just lost someone who cared about you so much, the best possible comfort can be the awareness that plenty of other people still care about you too. I felt so lonely and isolated after Dad died that I constantly wanted proof that other people loved me and were thinking about me.

You don't need to be intrusive to show you care. Sending a text at 3 p.m. on a random Tuesday saying you're thinking about them and that you love them is perfect. Popping a handwritten card in the post which says you're proud of how well they're coping is amazing. Just after Dad died, a girl I hadn't seen for ten years messaged me and appeared on my doorstep later that evening with a care package. She didn't want to come inside for a cup of tea or anything – she just wanted to give me a box filled with luxury cookies, a candle, bath stuff, and a good book. I was so moved I could have cried.

Don't stop including them (even if they say no!)

When they're grieving, a chasm seems to open up. They're feeling so much that putting it into words becomes almost impossible. That means they find it extremely difficult to respond to people – it's simply too exhausting. It's the same with activities too. For most of the first year after Dad's death, I found it really hard to leave the house. Once I arrived at a pub filled with my friends and had a severe panic attack as I walked through the door because the location felt so wrong to my grief-stricken mind.

Please don't stop inviting them to spend time with you. Even if they repeatedly say no, the knowledge that they're still being included (although they've put themselves on the back burner somewhat) helps to make them feel normal.

Be prepared for them to change fundamentally

I'm certain I am no longer the person I was when my mum was alive. I'm pretty sure that my dad's death meant I transitioned into yet another version of myself. I'm able to handle that in my own way, but the people

196

around me might have found that harder to accept.

There's every chance that such a monumental shift in their life could irrevocably change them as people. The dynamics of friendships and relationships may alter significantly, or even fail. In a perfect world, they'd love and appreciate all forms of support, but for many people, it can feel too much, too close, too complicated. If you're in the early stages of a relationship with a griever, be prepared for it to suddenly end – and you may never quite understand why.

If they want to talk about their grief or their loved one, let them

It's messy and complicated inside their heads, but putting grief into words gives it some sort of framework. It gets a little easier to comprehend, to see its edges. You might think it's not healthy for them to talk about death for hours and hours, but maybe that's what makes them feel better right now.

Sometimes, though, it's not a conversation about death in general that they want – it's simply to talk about the person they lost. And you can help! Ask questions about how their mum or dad used to behave. Bring up stories you remember about the person. Remind them that you also loved and remember them fondly.

Some of the loveliest messages I had after my parents' deaths were from old school friends I'd lost contact with who told me, "Your mum was always so interested in what we had to say! Those midnight feasts she made us! That time she told us to stop revising for mock exams and drove us to the Busted concert instead!" These are things I don't even remember, but it makes me so happy to know someone else does. Being told that someone else has memories of my mum is the most beautiful thing.

It's also important to make them aware that they can continue to talk to you about their grief. After the first year, it feels like the grief bubble starts to subside, and people don't mention it so much any more. But grief is an extremely long, drawn-out process, and they're always going to need some sort of support. Checking in at regular intervals throughout the span of your relationship is so valuable.

Recognise and champion their strength in grappling with this grief

Whenever one of my friends says they're proud of me for the way I've handled my parents' deaths, I feel ten feet tall. It never gets old. This grief is the toughest thing I've ever battled my way through – more hard

work and sheer determination than any school exam,
any sporting event, any work challenge, any breakup,
anything. It deserves to be recognised and
congratulated. Tell them they're doing amazingly.
Build them back up again.

13

Talking About Death

It doesn't matter whether you're the one who's grieving or whether you're supporting someone with their grief. The conversation around death is always an important one to have.

It's been two years since my dad died, and over a decade since Mum did. And yet most days I find myself thinking about death.

It's a secret, almost casual thought. When I'm on the bus, I idly imagine someone hitting me from behind. Invisible attackers are waiting around corners. I die in plane crashes and earthquakes and house fires. I die in a myriad of situations that I cannot control. This fear of my own demise is death anxiety: a common consequence of coping with the death of someone close to you. Bereavement causes us to confront our mortality, and it's a scary prospect.

Yet talking openly about grief and death is still avoided in the western world. We essentially live in a "death-denying" culture – which is why all the death admin is such a shock. For me, the unexpectedly positive side of dealing with death is that I find the subject a lot easier to talk about. More than that, talking about death is a release for me. It's cathartic. Getting deep into a conversation about the serious stuff allows my torrent of mixed-up emotions to spill out, and it turns my grief into something shareable and communal.

But every bereaved person is different. Some people prefer professional help, others can only speak to their family, whilst others cope best with support from strangers. For everyone else, death is a confusing, awkward and ultimately scary topic.

Many of us want to talk about death, but we don't know how to actually do it.

Why is death such a taboo subject?

Back in the Victorian era, grief was a public activity. People had huge funerals, posed photos were taken with the deceased, and widows used to wear black for a minimum of two years, sometimes for the rest of their lives. It alerted those around them to the sad circumstances, and grieving people were treated more gently by friends and strangers alike as a result.

Nowadays, British behaviour around death has completely changed. We've somehow made grief into a very private and personal experience, assuming that we need to stay out of the way and get on with it behind closed doors. But this attitude causes a huge amount of isolation. We steadfastly ignore the concept of death so much that it seems we're embarrassed by it. As a result, when someone dies we have very little idea of how to behave around those people who are grieving.

Nobody ever told me what losing my parents would feel like. Nobody explained how shellshocked I would be, how confused and isolated and traumatised my life would suddenly become. And nobody warned me that I might lose friends over it, or that other people might find it hard to cope with my bereavement too.

When I went back to university a few weeks after my mum's death, the reactions I encountered were extraordinary. One girl who lived in my shared student house didn't speak to me for months and avoided being in the same room as me – apparently because she "didn't know what to say". I felt like a leper. A couple of years later, I told the guy I'd been casually dating for a few weeks that Mum had died and he never spoke to me again. I felt as if I'd done something wrong, even while I was still grieving for her loss. People tend to forget that death is the most natural thing in the world because our culture is so intent on hiding it from us.

Ten years on, I'm more understanding of these types of reactions. Death and grief are seriously scary topics, and if you've got an anxious personality then your thought processes can spiral – particularly if you haven't directly experienced dealing with a death. But ultimately, this still doesn't sit right with me. If there's one thing we can be certain of, it's that we are all going to die. Before then, we'll almost certainly have to cope with the death of someone close to us. So why aren't we preparing ourselves earlier for the emotional impact of this grief? Why are we pretending it won't hurt until we discover, too late, how much it does?

Why it's important to talk about death

From an emotional standpoint, it's important to acknowledge that death is a real and inevitable fact of life. I know being reminded of our own mortality can be upsetting, but addressing the idea of death also takes away its shock value. If you haven't talked about death before, you could well be shocked by the physical changes in someone who's dying, the conversations you or they might suddenly want to have as the end draws near, or the feelings which could overwhelm you during the process.

It's also precisely when you need the support of the people closest to you. During the fortnight when my mum was dying, my house remained virtually empty. This isn't necessarily either a good or a bad thing. I just didn't know I was allowed to ask people to be there for me. I was twenty years old. My dad's way of coping was to keep things private, and I went along with his decision. But it meant that when my mum died I felt like an outsider in too many situations. I knew my tears would drag a conversation down and make people feel awkward, but I also knew I couldn't avoid talking about what had happened. It was too all-consuming, and it wasn't fair to me or her memory.

So when I first heard that my dad was going into hospital and it wasn't looking good, the first thing I did was message my closest friends. I needed them to know so that they could help me carry this weight. Choosing to immediately share what was happening emboldened me to start asking for the other sources of help Dad needed – making phone calls to solicitors and hospitals and palliative care teams – but it also reminded me that people actually cared. I realised that Dad and I mattered enough for people to go out of their way to make sure we were OK – well, as OK as we could be. And I felt I wasn't quite so alone.

Then there's the purely logistical side of discussing death. Over 50% of British people haven't drawn up a will. They haven't told anyone where they'd like to be buried or if they'd prefer cremation or what songs they'd like at the funeral. They haven't told anyone their online passwords or what happens to their diaries or revealed the existence of all that hereditary jewellery hidden in the attic. Although I managed to deal with all the admin surrounding Dad's death, I still knew nothing about the necessary official processes. Google was an absolute lifesaver, but even that couldn't take away the fact that I was doing all this for the first time while dealing with the worst emotional phase of my life.

Coping with death and grief when you've got no guidebook can make you think you're going crazy – but it doesn't have to be this way. There are easy, tangible ways we can talk about death.

Talk to your friends

I'm very lucky that none of my closest friends shy away from discussing death with me – although to be fair they've had ten years of me bringing up the topic! Some have also lost parents or people close to them.

That doesn't make them automatically keen to talk. However, they know it's important to me and they want to help. Factor in a bottle of red wine and it's that much easier to open up.

Talk to your family

It might be a sensitive topic, but it's highly recommended to at least have a preliminary conversation with your immediate family about death, so you know what their thoughts and feelings are.

Talk to a therapist

When someone close to you dies, it's often assumed that you'll go to therapy. As I mentioned in Chapter 10, I firmly believe that therapy is only going to help if you're the one who wants to be there. If you've got no desire to talk through your emotions with a virtual stranger in a tiny room with a box of tissues on the table, then there's every chance it will just make you feel more alone.

Once you feel the need to seek out a therapist for yourself, these are the most common options in the UK:

Therapy through the NHS

Go to your local doctor's office and talk about your options for grief and bereavement care. The good news is these services are free, but they might involve long waiting times.

Therapy through your local council

If you've suffered a bereavement you can usually find support from your local council – either one-to-one grief support sessions or groups. I applied through my council's website and received a call from a support worker, who then referred me to an online CBT course. I didn't find this particularly useful because I'd already started going to private CBT therapy sessions, but it was good to have another resource to hand.

Therapy through a charity or hospice

My dad was at a fantastic hospice and they offered us sessions with a family worker, both during his decline and after his death. Charities like Cruse and Marie Curie also offer bereavement counselling.

Private therapy

If you're willing to pay for therapy, there are probably

hundreds of therapists in your local area. I used www.counselling-directory.org.uk and read through profiles until I found a few I liked, then sent them an email explaining my history and went on from there.

Talk on the phone to an organisation

If you'd rather not meet face-to-face, there are several helplines you can phone for a chat. In the UK, charities like Samaritans (116 123, open 24 hours), Mind (0300 123 3393 or text 86463), and Marie Curie (0800 090 2309) have dedicated phone lines for you to call and discuss whatever's on your mind.

Talk to other people

At some point in your grief journey, you might suddenly feel compelled to talk at length about death and dying. This happened to me once I started going to therapy: I had so much to say about grief that I actively wanted to find spaces where this was possible, even if it was just with strangers! Luckily, there are plenty of support groups and organisations running events about bereavement and loss. To find out what's available in your local area, try asking for information at hospitals, hospices, churches and funeral homes, or look on meetup.com (there are over 500 groups relating to grief, with 68,000 members), or simply Google a phrase like "grief support near me."

Grief communities are springing up all over the world too, from grief podcasts to loss meet-ups to death dinner parties. A huge number of grievers want to connect with other people who've faced this challenge of monumental loss – and many of us are realising that if those spaces don't exist, we need to make them ourselves.

For me, writing online about my grief has been a wonderful way to realise just how many people want to share their stories. Whenever I publish something I receive comments and private messages from others who've suffered similar losses – but I didn't move this kind of connection into my offline world until 2018.

Go to a loss meet-up

My first experience of a community grief-space was with Let's Talk About Loss, a UK-based organisation which runs meet-ups for 16-30 year olds who've been bereaved (@letstalkaboutloss on Twitter and Instagram). Let's Talk About Loss currently runs meet-ups in over twenty locations, and plans to keep on expanding.

I attended their launch in central London and then went to their first event, where at least thirty people gathered in the cosy lobby of a central London cinema. I'll be honest – this was the first time I'd actively discussed my personal grief with a group of strangers who'd suffered in the same way. I was so nervous that I walked past the door three times before summoning the courage to go inside. Once I did, I immediately found a group of like-minded people to talk to – and there was honest-to-goodness screaming of delight when two sisters learned I'd lost both my parents, just like they had. It was a surreal experience to sit with a group of people my age who'd all lost their parents, friends, partners, or siblings, and to bond over the feelings we shared.

Go to a Death Cafe

The Death Cafe (www.deathcafe.com) is a global network of meet-ups with a very simple concept: drink tea, eat cake, and discuss death. I've been to one session so far, where I drank tea with strangers in a Buddhist centre in south London. Although most people were attending because they'd lost someone, I enjoyed chatting about the actual concept of death for once, instead of delving into my own personal experiences.

Find other people in your networks who've

been bereaved

When I talk to people who've been through the same kind of loss as I have, you can't shut us up. We're eagerly and excitedly comparing experiences, mutually commiserating over the emotional minefield we've both gone through, and making the dark-humoured jokes only we can make. Realising other people know exactly what I mean makes me feel so much less alone. You don't have to look for these conversations only at "death" meet-ups either. The chances are that lots of your friends and acquaintances have lost people close to them too.

Since I began to speak publicly about grief, I've become curiously adept at finding the bereaved - from old classmates to friends' housemates to internet commenters. Most people really do want to talk about grief and death – they just need to find the right person or the right vocabulary to allow them permission.

14

Finding Your Grief Language

Discovering there are so many spaces where we're able to talk about death can be a relief to many of us. Unfortunately though, because discussing death is culturally taboo, we don't have a clearly defined death vocabulary to rely on. Most people have no real clue what words to use when talking about death – and if you're the one who's grieving, you're often expected to lead the conversation. Except you're just as inept as everyone else.

Normal language feels insufficient for expressing your grief. It's too much to explain in mere words. That in itself may feel extremely distressing, as if you're even more alone, so it often causes pure emotion to come out instead: screaming, crying, shouting. Pain and sadness express themselves through action when the words aren't there. Despite being a writer, I've often wished I could just hold out my brain for people to look at, so that I wouldn't have to try and explain what I was going through. If they could just see it for themselves, that would save me the struggle.

Despite the limitations, it's important to find your own grief language. If you can recognise which words resonate with you and which phrases you never want to hear again, it can help significantly with the way you talk about grief.

Which words make you feel uncomfortable to hear?

Everyone has certain words or phrases which are particularly painful – and I don't just mean the obvious ones like "They're in a better place" or "They wouldn't want you to be sad." After Mum's death, I tensed up whenever someone said I was "really strong" for what I'd been through. It made me want to lash out. Did they honestly think I'd had a choice in how I'd behaved? Yet ironically, when Dad died I *did* want someone to tell me I was strong because I felt I'd completely fallen apart! The phrase which particularly frustrated me after his death was "It's going to be OK." My logical mind raged at this because the speaker seemed to be bypassing my current grief state to

imagine me when I was better – a state I couldn't
envisage reaching.

And yet I barely mentioned how uncomfortable
these phrases made me.

I've met grieving people who seemed happy
enough to talk about death until I unknowingly used
their "trigger word" and they suddenly shut down. In
these moments I've wondered whether they knew
beforehand that this word or phrase would trigger
them, or if it was an unwelcome surprise. Of course,
it's not really practical to hand out a list of words that
people can't say around you – but if you're already
aware of them, it can reduce their impact.

Which words do you use to describe the death you've experienced?

There's no escaping the fact that people will often ask
about the circumstances of death. Whether or not you
feel obliged to answer, the question itself can be
upsetting. If you have a set way of responding though,
it can make all the difference. I spent eight years
repeating the same sentence, almost on autopilot, to
explain what had happened to my mum. Then when
Dad died I had to amend it, creating a new soundbite:

My mum died when I was twenty – she'd had cancer ten

years earlier but then it came back, and she died pretty quickly after that – and my dad had fibrosis for two years, and died when I was twenty-nine.

When people hear me say this for the first time they react with surprise and sadness. They say how sorry they are; their faces fall. But I cope remarkably well – because I'm now so used to explaining how my parents died that these words no longer impact me the way they used to. I've become numb to them.

Are you repeating the same descriptive words?

Certain words will resonate with your experience of grief, so you store them up and reuse them. For me, it's words like "visceral", "overwhelming", and "animalistic" – in fact, you've probably noticed them more than once throughout this book! In the early days of grief, these words were almost totemic: I felt animalistic with my crying on a near-daily basis, my emotions were always overwhelming, and I felt deeply, viscerally connected to how my body felt during the hardest moments of grief.

Looking back, I think these particular words were both a comfort and a source of fear. I wanted desperately to encapsulate my grief in words so I could contain it, and these words felt like familiar signposts to get through the storm. And now that I describe grief with these same words, they have much less power over me.

It's OK to invent words if they help you explain your grief better

If there aren't any words which fully convey how you feel, make them up. You're absolutely allowed. It can be as simple as hyphenating "grief" or "death" with literally any word – like "grief-fog", which I use to explain the foggy mindset you often find yourself in, a "death-iversary" for the dates on which my parents died, and "grief-weight", which explains why my weight changed significantly after Dad's death. An internet favourite is "grief bacon". This comes from the German word *kummerspeck* which essentially means "eating when you're sad". The online publication Modern Loss loves this word so much that they made an entire category of "grief bacon" articles!

It may feel silly, but I think it's important to give names to these parts of the grief process. It gives them validity and helps to structure what you're going through. It also makes it easier to explain what's happening to other people – and plenty of fellow grievers will empathise, as they recognise these feelings too.

15

Afterwards

A few months after my mum died, I realised that I now saw my life up to that point totally differently. It felt like those twenty years with Mum had been a dress rehearsal for my real life - a life which would no longer include her. I was so scared of what it would look like and feel like. For a while, I didn't even want to know.

You may feel like your life has stopped along with theirs. But it hasn't.

When Mum died, I thought my situation was completely unique. I thought I was totally alone. I thought nobody would ever understand what I'd been through, or how I felt. But by the time Dad died, I'd already spent nine years of my grief journey learning that I had an immediate bond with complete strangers because they'd lost a parent too. As I met these people and heard stories which echoed my own, I started realising that, for better or worse, I have the companionship of thousands of others around the world who understand me on this specific emotional level. And so do you.

The strange positive to grief is that it brings unlikely people together. When you meet other members of The Adult Orphan Club, you can somehow skip all the usual pleasantries and dive straight into intense, personal, vulnerable conversations with people who truly get it. Dealing with death is one of the biggest emotions we have to face, but talking about it doesn't have to be all doom and gloom. It just gives us permission to be sad and vulnerable about the complex emotions we all feel surrounding death. For me, the scariest thing about death is that it highlights how easy it is to find yourself alone and isolated in your own feelings. But it's important to remember that talking about death doesn't make it happen any quicker. It just allows us to feel less scared and more prepared.

Sometimes I feel strangely lucky that I've had to confront death so early on in my life because I know now that I'm able to cope with anything. I've lived through watching both my parents die and I've come out the other side – battered and bruised but ultimately OK. That said, I haven't magically "recovered" from grieving. I carry my parents with me every day. I'm still learning how to manage the sadness in a way which keeps me upright, instead of breaking me down. And yet, after ten years of holding so much of this grief inside, I can't tell you how cathartic and freeing and joyful it feels to share my grief with you on these pages. It's like I've lifted a weight from my shoulders.

All deaths are different. All grief responses are different too. But however alone you feel within those differences, I promise you're not. Not really. The bizarre, bittersweet beauty of death is that it reminds us we're fundamentally the same. We all have to face loss alongside the privilege of being able to live life.

The most important message you can take away from this book is that you don't have to keep these emotions bottled up inside. So I hope you'll accept my invitation to share some of your grief. It can be with me, or a family member, or a good friend. It could be sending your first email to a therapist, or finding a community meet-up with others in your area who are grieving.

There are so many ways to share the burden of your

grief a little – and there are so many people who are ready to hear you.

I'm one of them.

Resources

I've used the online world for so much of my grief support, but it can be hard to know where to look. Here are some of the resources I've found to be most helpful.

End of life care

There are many turbulent Google searches conducted in the dead of night or in snatched moments outside a hospital ward. I recommend going to the most trusted sources first: they lay out the requisite information simply and calmly. For UK readers, the NHS guidelines for end of life care (www.nhs.uk/conditions/end-of-life-care/) is a good place to start, as is Hospice UK's guide (www.hospiceuk.org/about-hospice-care/what-is-hospice-care). For international readers, try searching key words like "end of life care," "terminal care," and "hospice care" alongside the name of your government and/or biggest health organisation, and go from there.

Grief admin

The sheer volume of legal processes required after a death can feel unending. The UK government's website has a step-by-step guide which details the official process of what to do after someone dies, including the relevant organisations you need to contact (www.gov.uk/after-a-death). Using their Tell Us Once service will report a death to various departments of central and local government (including taxes, public pension, passport, driving licence, council tax, and removal from the electoral register). To remove your loved one's name and address from mailing lists, use the Deceased Preference Service (www.deceasedpreferenceservice.co.uk) and The Bereavement Register (www.thebereavementregister.org.uk) – they quickly reduce the amount of unwanted marketing and junk mail. For general guidance about all aspects of grief admin, The Bereavement Advice Centre has plenty of helpful resources (www.bereavementadvice.org).

Probate

Probate – the legal procedure of authenticating and administering someone's will – is different in every country. In the UK, you should first check the government's official probate information (www.gov.uk/wills-probate-inheritance), then read up on probate and estate administration in more simplified language at Bereavement Advice (www.bereavementadvice.org). If you need help with inheritance tax, Money Service Advice (www.moneyadviceservice.org.uk) has a good guide to the topic, and the forums on Money Saving Expert are helpful for all kinds of things including the transfer of house ownership (forums.moneysavingexpert.com).

Help and support for mental health

When my dad was diagnosed as terminal, I saved the number for the Samaritans in my phone – but it still took a few months before I felt desperate enough to call them. When I finally did, the woman who answered was calm and friendly, completely without judgement. There are several listening services that you can call in a crisis – I suggest keeping these helpline numbers in your phone, just in case.

Mind: 0300 123 3393 (or text 86463)

Cruse Bereavement Care: 0808 808 1677

Marie Curie: 0800 090 2309

Anxiety UK: 03444 775 774

Samaritans: 116 123 (helpline is open 24 hours)

Childline: 0800 1111

Therapy

There are many different types of therapy and it can seem somewhat overwhelming to start looking for it. In the UK, you're likely to be signposted one of four ways: seeking therapy via referral from your doctor, through self-referral at a charity, hospice or third sector organisation, through your place of work or education, or with a private therapist. Most of these therapies will be free or low-cost, except for private therapy.

If you choose to pay for private therapy, the cost will vary depending on a therapist's experience and location (i.e. London-based therapists are usually more expensive). Sessions are usually between £40-£80 per 50 minute session. It can also be overwhelming to narrow down the options – for instance, I decided I'd most like to work with a female therapist who was relatively close in age to me, and I was most drawn to those who seemed open, creative and kind on their profiles. You can search for therapists on the following sites:

CBT Register: an online register of officially credited therapists specialising in CBT (www.cbtregisteruk.com).

Counselling Directory: a UK-wide database of professional counsellors and therapists (www.counselling-directory.org.uk).

The British Association for Counselling and Psychotherapy (BACP): a nationwide directory of trained professionals where you can search for someone suitable for your needs (www.bacp.co.uk).

Books

There's a multitude of grief-related literature available, but these are some of the books which resonated most with me. I'd also suggest looking at the lists on Goodreads and Amazon to see what other people have recommended.

- *With The End In Mind* by Kathryn Mannix
- *The Year of Magical Thinking* by Joan Didion
- *H is for Hawk* by Helen Macdonald
- *Splitting the Difference: A Heart-Shaped Memoir*

by Tre Rodriguez Miller
- *The Iceberg: A Memoir* by Marion Coutts
- *A Grief Observed* by C.S. Lewis
- *I Am, I Am, I Am: Seventeen Brushes With Death* by Maggie O'Farrell
- *A Manual For Heartache* by Cathy Rentzenbrink
- *Grief is the Thing with Feathers* by Max Porter
- *When Breath Becomes Air* by Paul Kalanithi
- *The Wild Other: A Memoir* by Clover Stroud
- *Travelling with Ghosts: A Memoir* by Shannon Leone Fowler
- *The Last Act of Love: The Story of My Brother and His Sister* by Cathy Rentzenbrink

Grief, loss, and bereavement accounts to follow online

Social media can be a lifeline during the grief process, and these accounts have all been particularly helpful for me.

Dying Matters: an organisation raising awareness and encouraging open conversation around dying, death and bereavement (www.dyingmatters.org).

The Good Grief Trust: a UK-based charity providing

support and reassurance for the bereaved (www.thegoodgrieftrust.org).

Modern Loss: a website filled with candid conversation, resources and community on grief and loss (www.modernloss.com).

Living Well Dying Well: a not-for-profit association for End of Life doulas working to change the face of death and dying in the UK (www.eol-doula.uk).

The Griefcast: an award-winning podcast about grief and death, hosted by comedian Cariad Lloyd (www.cariadlloyd.com/griefcast).

The Griefcase: a monthly meet up group in London, UK, with a focus on the creative ways we interpret grief. Poppy Chancellor also hosts grief-focused sessions with guests on Instagram Live (www.instagram.com/thegriefcase).

Let's Talk About Loss: a support network for bereaved young people aged 16-30, hosting meet up groups across the UK (www.letstalkaboutloss.org).

Death Cafe: global events for people who'd like to talk about death in a relaxed setting (www.deathcafe.com).

Flora Baker

Acknowledgements

To Mike and Ben – for reading my first drafts and giving such considered and wonderfully positive words of encouragement and feedback.

To my editor Liz Hedgecock, designer Vanessa Lovegrove and proofreader Emily Buchanan – you've all been stars, and I'm so glad we've been able to work together.

To the young orphans of WhatsApp – I'm constantly amazed by the collective strength in our little chat window. You're all incredible.

To the blogging community – our joyfully raucous times (particularly in Trentino, Antigua, and Berlin) reminded me I still had a life and a personality outside of the grief.

To my wonderful friends – particularly Kim, Helena, and Nicki. Thanks for giving me the space to talk through my grief over countless bottles of red.

To Lainey – for being my mum's oldest friend and my parents' constant champion. Our annual reunions in Charing Cross mean the world to me.

To Ros and Carol – for stepping in as surrogate parents when I needed you the most. Whether it's dinner by the fire in Trafalgar Square or a cup of tea at the kitchen table, you've given me a continuation of the love my parents had for me. I couldn't ask for anything more.

To my closest girls – Mimi, Chee, Lucy, Emi, Rachel, and Jas. You're my chosen family, my sisters, and I'm so very grateful for your friendship, your voice notes and your unwavering love and support.

To the hundreds of people who've sent me their own stories of loss and grief – thank you for your honesty, vulnerability and bravery in sharing the deepest parts of yourselves with me. I wouldn't have written this book if I hadn't realised there was such a need for companionship through the loneliness of all this.

And most importantly, to my wonderful mum and dad – you taught me the importance of words, and you gave me a voice. I still hear yours wherever I go. I hope you knew how much I loved you both. I always will.

Flora Baker
May 2020

About the Author

Flora Baker is a freelance writer and adult orphan from London, UK. After studying American Literature and Creative Writing at both the University of East Anglia (UEA) in Norwich and SFSU in San Francisco, she travelled the world for five years before resettling in London to care for her terminally ill father. She now lives in her family house along with her parents' overflowing bookshelves, a growing collection of houseplants and (soon, hopefully) an adopted cat. *The Adult Orphan Club* is her first book.

Flora writes online about travel, grief and mental health, and loves to discuss these topics with her readers. You can find her on Twitter and Instagram at @FloraBaker and read more of her writing at the award-winning www.floratheexplorer.com.

Before you go...

Why not leave a review?

Thank you so much for reading *The Adult Orphan Club*. I'm so glad you chose it, and hope you found it useful in some way.

If you enjoyed the book, please consider sharing it with your friends and family, posting on Twitter and Facebook, or leaving a review on Amazon or Goodreads. Every review helps more people find the book, and I appreciate your feedback and support so much.

Please say hello!

If you have questions or stories you'd like to share, I'd love to hear from you on my blog (floratheexplorer.com), on Instagram or on Twitter (@FloraBaker). To keep up to date with my grief writing, sign up to my email list at floratheexplorer.com/newsletter.

Made in the USA
Monee, IL
26 February 2021